"Mrs. Caruana has captured the basic organizational methods for developing efficiency not only with homeschooling, but with everyday disciplines for havin̶ ... excellent book that will be must reading for those inv̶ ... ̶ ̶ homeschooling alternative."

... founder of More Hours in My Day

"A useful guide for every homeschooler, whether she falls into the 'organizationally-challenged' or the 'already well-organized' category. Covers how to organize your thoughts, your time, your space and loads more. Best of all it offers *manageable* techniques for everyone."

—MAUREEN MCCAFFREY,
Homeschooling Today Magazine

"As a mother of five who homeschooled for seven years, I only wish I had this book earlier! It is filled with practical methods to evaluate the reasons for clutter. Better yet, Vicki offers easy-to-follow *solutions* to these problems. This is a must read for all homeschoolers who want to spend less time shuffling papers and more time teaching."

—ELLIE KAY, best-selling author of
Shop, Save and Share and
How to Save Money Every Day

"I am truly impressed with Vicki's comprehensive and complete grasp on the organizational hurdles in a homeschool home. This is a must read for all household CEOs and home educators."

—LANE JORDAN, author of
12 Steps to Becoming a More Organized Woman

Other Books by Vicki Caruana
Apples & Chalkdust
(Honor Books, 1998)

Success in School
(Focus Publishing, 2000)

Apples & Chalkdust for Teachers
(Honor Books, 2000)

The ABCs of Homeschooling
(Crossway Books, 2001)

Apples & Chalkdust #2
(River Oak Publishers, 2001)

The
Organized
Home
Schooler

VICKI CARUANA

CROSSWAY BOOKS • WHEATON, ILLINOIS
A DIVISION OF GOOD NEWS PUBLISHERS

The Organized Homeschooler

Copyright © 2001 by Vicki Caruana

Published by Crossway Books
        a division of Good News Publishers
        1300 Crescent Street
        Wheaton, Illinois 60187

Cover design: Cindy Kiple

First printing, 2001

Printed in the United States of America

Scripture taken from the *Holy Bible: New International Version*, © 1973, 1978, 1984 by International Bible Society. Used by permission of Zondervan Publishing House. All rights reserved.

The "NIV" and "New International Version" trademarks are registered in the United States Patent and Trademark Office by International Bible Society. Use of either trademark requires the permission of International Bible Society.

Library of Congress Cataloging-in-Publication Data
Caruana, Vicki.
   The organized homeschooler / Vicki Caruana.
      p.   cm.
   ISBN 1-58134-305-1 (TPB : alk. paper)
   1. Home schooling—Planning. 2. School management and organization.
   3. Christian education—Home training. I. Title
LC40.C378   2001
371.04'2'068—dc21   2001003933
                                             CIP

15	14	13	12	11	10	09	08	07	06	05	04	03	02	01
15	14	13	12	11	10	9	8	7	6	5	4	3	2	1

*This book is dedicated to all the homeschoolers who
unashamedly raise their hands in my workshops
to say that they are disorganized.
I pray it ministers to you.*

*I want to thank my husband, Chip,
who has lived for me a more organized life and
has modeled and taught me so much of what is in this book.
As I read this book, I sometimes hear
his voice more than my own.*

Table of Contents

Introduction

People marvel at how organized our home is. They even peek into our cupboards just hoping a mess is inside. They're usually disappointed. I believe that there is always room for improvement when it comes to being organized. I have not "arrived" by any stretch of the imagination, but I'm well on my way.

When we decided to bring our children home to school, I was suddenly faced with more organizational challenges than ever before. At first I tried to order things the way I did when I had my own classroom as a public school teacher. The more I tried to make our homeschool look and feel like a classroom, the more frustrated and disappointed I became. There was a definite flaw in my system.

My goal was to have what we needed when we needed it and to have my children just as able to maintain that order as I. After my trial and error we arrived at what works for us. This book doesn't outline our system for you. It presents a way of thinking that will encourage you to seek out what will work for your family and will give you the courage to do it.

When homeschool friends would see our system, they would quickly ask what I did to keep things so orderly. I found myself training people every time they came to visit. But there were a few women who, even though they seemed desperate to be organized, failed at every attempt. What I discovered was that their desire for organization was not deep-rooted. It was a shallow attempt at fitting into an orderly world. The bottom line? They didn't really feel the need to be organized. They just didn't want to look disorganized to outsiders. That was when I realized that organization is a matter of the heart.

Whenever I am faced with a challenge, I run to the Word of God to seek guidance. What, if anything, did God have to say about being organized? "Seek and ye shall find." God is far from silent on living an orderly life with purpose and deliberateness. He waits to bless you! Find out what God is like, and you'll discover what He wants for you.

Our God is a God of order and purpose. He does nothing without purpose!

1

The Heart of the Matter

There is surely a future hope for you, and your hope will not be cut off.

—PROVERBS 23:18

You picked up this book *hoping* for answers. You *hope* it will help you find a way to relieve your anxiety about your current state of affairs. You *hope* to find reflections of your own life to which you can readily relate. I *hope* this for you as well! The premise of this book is that becoming more organized is first a matter of the heart. Our actions come as a result of what is in our hearts. Our desires determine our steps. So before we can truly change *how* we do things, we should consider *why* we do things the way we do them. The second premise is that you *can* become a more organized homeschooler, even if you are already quite discouraged. You can because you can do all things through Him who gives you strength (Philippians 4:13).

Within the pages of this book, you will find practical guidelines for becoming a more organized homeschooler. I will share with you what works for our family, but I caution you not to assume that there is one best way to be organized. Every family is different, with different personalities and needs. I don't promise that my way will work for you. Instead I invite you on a journey to find out for yourself what works and what doesn't. Come with me as we travel toward that final end. Yet, just as on a journey, there should be time for planning and consideration of the route. There might be opportunity for diversion, and there will be moments of inevitable delay, but reaching the final destination will not be lost.

Your desire to become a more organized homeschooler is one that is pleasing to God. Be encouraged! He has already equipped you to do what is pleasing to Him (Hebrews 13:21). It will take wisdom to choose actions that will lead to a more orderly life. Pray for that wisdom, and He will be faithful to give it to you. On this journey to becoming a more organized homeschooler, make your requests known to God as your first step. Pray with the confidence that He will perfect you. Remember that He has already begun a good work in you and will perfect it in you until the day of Christ Jesus (Philippians 1:6).

MY JOURNEY

Having said this, I confess that my own journey to a more orderly life has been filled with delays, detours, pitfalls, and distractions. I am still en route. It is a process. And I can't do it alone. When I was growing up, I rejected any help my mother offered to be orderly. The oldest of five children, unusually blessed with my own bedroom, I was a mess! My mother chose not to engage in this particular battle of the wills. Her solution? Close my bedroom door! It didn't matter that my two sisters, who shared a room, were immaculate. Their sense of order did not rub off on me. After all, why would I want to be like them? My mother's periodic comments— gentle reminders like "I always know where you've been"—didn't seem to make an impact either. I do admit that if a friend was coming over, I would quickly and efficiently clean my bedroom. But it was only a matter of hours before it again looked as if a bomb exploded. I felt no need to be more organized.

I spent a lot of time in my room, and I think that contributed to its messy state. I rarely attended activities outside my home, and friends spent more time at my house than the other way around. Now as a homeschooler I realize that much of the challenge of becoming or staying organized is due to the fact that we are all home much of the time. Houses don't get nearly as messy if you aren't home.

It wasn't until I went to college and lived in a dorm that things changed. My roommate was even messier than me! The sleeping area was a complete disaster all the time. The study area couldn't be found due to the piles on top of piles. And there was half-eaten food to be found under, inside, and on top of many of those piles. I never felt comfortable there. I chose to study at the library until it closed and worked enough hours during the week that I wouldn't have to do anything but sleep in my dorm room. Unfortunately, sleep was elusive because the room was not a soothing place to be.

For the first time in my life I wanted a change. My solution? I became orderly almost overnight. It was like quitting smoking cold turkey. For me it was the best way. I hate confrontations; so instead of encouraging my roommate to straighten up, I made sure my half of the room was orderly. I realized that I could only take care of myself and that I couldn't put a desire in her that just wasn't there.

I believe the same is true for you as you read this book. I can't wave a wand and *poof*, you're organized. I also can't climb inside your heart and put the desire to be more orderly inside you. I can share with you what I've learned and encourage you on your own journey, but I won't lead or drag you along the way. After all, it's your journey.

WHERE ARE YOU ON YOUR JOURNEY?

The Bible is the authority on how we should live. There is no problem or challenge that cannot be answered with Scripture. God's Word should be your first source of strength and reference as you journey. God knows you better than you know yourself (see Psalm 139:1-18). Before you begin this journey, let's see what kind of traveler you are.

• You may be reading this as an already discouraged and organizationally impaired person. If you feel weak, rest in the fact that God will glorify Himself in your weakness. Be assured that any competence you gain comes from Him (2 Corinthians 3:5).

• You may be reading this because you have good intentions about becoming more organized, yet cannot (Romans 7:18). You're trying so hard to follow the law of the organized that you feel defeated on all sides. You're afraid that you will fail once again in your quest. But God did not give you a spirit of timidity but of power and love and self-discipline (2 Timothy 1:7).

• Finally, you may be reading this because you already take pride in your organizational skills and are looking for more ways to improve them. Be careful. Your pride may lead to disgrace (Proverbs 11:2). Instead, use your gifts to minister to others (1 Peter 4:10). You may be the mentor that God wants to use in someone else's life. Look for such opportunities. Remember to "be completely humble and gentle; be patient, bearing with one another in love" (Ephesians 4:2).

These are all matters of the heart. Try first to recognize where you are on the journey, and trust that God will grow you up to be like Him (Ephesians 4:15). That is the real journey! That's the race we all want to finish well.

THE HEART, MIND, BODY CONNECTION

Sheer determination and confidence in your own ability will not make the changes you seek. The world says, "Put your mind to it—mind over matter—it's all in your head." A famous athletic shoe company tells us to "Just do it!" We are surrounded by voices that tell us if we think right, we'll do right. But it doesn't begin with our thoughts; it begins with our hearts. Throughout Scripture we are reminded that believing is what saves. Believing is not thinking. Thinking is head knowledge. Believing is heart knowledge. But even as Christians we fall into the trap of believing it's all in our heads.

We do what we think, and we think because of what we believe. I firmly believe that becoming a more organized home-schooler begins in the heart. Before beginning the journey to becoming more organized, it is important that we all have a clear starting point. You know in your heart where this starting point is for you. You can now make thoughtful choices that will spur you on your way.

MIND MATTERS

If we are using Scripture as our road map, we can memorize the way or refer to it periodically as we journey. With regard to becoming a more organized homeschooler, consider these mile markers on the way. Look up these verses, and then jot down a few thoughts about how each applies to your journey toward organization.

• Proverbs 13:16

_____

_____

• Proverbs 14:15

_____

_____

• Proverbs 16:9

_____

_____

• Proverbs 19:2

_____

_____

• Proverbs 22:3

_____

_____

• Proverbs 24:27

_____

_____

Study is one way we order our thoughts. Consider the following words, and do a Bible word study using a resource such as *Vine's Expository Dictionary*. This is an excellent activity to do with your children as well.

• Prudent

_____

_____

• Haste

_____

_____

• Order or orderly

_____

_____

• Confusion or lawlessness

_____

_____

BODY MATTERS

What can we do with the heart and mind matters we've learned thus far? Even educational psychologists agree that many of us learn by doing. Some of the ideas listed below can be done as you, the parent alone, continue on your journey. Some can be done with your children, so they too learn the way. Remember that there is joy in the journey!

- Save your money for a special purchase or project. Determine how long it should take to save the required amount.
- Make a list of tasks that could be done in a day. Prioritize the tasks, from least important to most.
- Make a list of homeschool curricula you currently own.
- Design a project with a deadline. List all elements of the project, and schedule your time in order to finish by the deadline.
- Read *Clutter's Last Stand* by Don Aslett (Writer's Digest Books, 1984). Take notes, and implement ideas from the book.
- Study the chapter "Planning and Priorities" in Wayne Mack's book *A Homework Manual for Biblical Living*, Volume 1 (P & R Publishing, 1980).

These are just a few of the ideas to help you do what you think based upon what you believe. They are adapted from *Plants Grown Up* by Pam Forster (DoorPosts, 1995). The manual *For Instruction in Righteousness* is also a bountiful resource for you as you make this journey with your children.

FOLLOW THE PATH

It's difficult sometimes to know which way we should go. We don't always understand what makes one way better than the other. But God knows! As you journey you may get discouraged. You may question whether or not this is the way you should go. Ask God now to direct your path. The following verses will help you.

• Psalm 119:35: "Direct me in the path of your commands, for there I find delight."

• Psalm 119:104: "I gain understanding from your precepts; therefore I hate every wrong path."

• Psalm 119:105: "Your word is a lamp to my feet and a light for my path."

• Proverbs 2:9: "Then [when God gives you wisdom] you will understand what is right and just and fair—every good path."

There are dangers when you stray from the path. You can know you are on the wrong path if you become anxious, confused, full of despair, fearful, even angry. Do you feel any of these right now? If you do, you are experiencing the consequences of living a disorderly life. You already know firsthand that disorganization conveys only negative ideas. The following are associated with it: ailment, anarchy, bedlam, chaos, complaint, confusion, disease, disorder, lawlessness, malady, mess, pandemonium, trouble, turbulence, uproar, violence, etc. In a nutshell, disorganization is not a good thing!

• Disorganization leads to disorder.

Disorder is defined as "a lack of order or regular arrangement; confusion." Does this describe your surroundings? Not being able to find what you need when you need it may be a normal state in your house. Often items are never returned to where they belong, if they even have a home. There is no logical placement for your stuff. You never know where your keys are. You know when you live among disorder. It is never a good feeling to be disorderly. And you are frustrated that your children can't seem to keep their rooms straight either. Somehow you thought they would magically pick up better habits than you did.

The opposite of disorder is *order*. It comes from the word *taxis* and is a desirable condition. Paul wrote to the Colossians, "For though I am absent from you in body, I am present with you in spirit and delight to see how orderly you are and how firm your faith in Christ is" (2:5).

• Disorganization creates chaos.

Chaos is defined as "utter confusion and disorder." Disorder leads to chaos. Many scientists believe that order will eventually come out of chaos, as in (according to their theories) the creation of the universe. But that doesn't take into account intelligent design. Your home and school are your "universe." You have the benefit of intelligent design. So order certainly can be drawn out of chaos, but that doesn't happen all by itself.

The opposite of chaos is *coordination* or *system*. Both words imply intelligent design. Someone must take responsibility if order is to be restored. "We know that in all things God works for the good of those who love him, who have been called according to his purpose" (Romans 8:28). Things don't just happen to work together for good—God works them.

• Disorganization causes stress.

Stress is defined as "a factor causing mental or emotional strain or tension." It is difficult to have peace in your home or inside yourself when you live under stress. Have you found yourself stressed by the amount of paperwork your homeschool generates? It piles up and piles up and at some point you think you'll put it all together into a portfolio. But when the time comes, you're overwhelmed and instead toss it all in the trash. Yes, you feel guilty, but now you're less stressed because of the absence of those paper piles. In contrast, not only *can* you organize those piles in a productive and purposeful manner, but creating order in your homeschool will alleviate unnecessary and harmful stress.

The opposite of stress is *peace*, which comes from the Greek word *eirene*. It is mentioned 230 times in the Bible! Christ came to impart God's peace. "For God is not a God of disorder but of peace"

(1 Corinthians 14:33). Our God is a God of order and purpose. If anyone can help bring peace into your home, He can!

As you read through this book, you will be challenged to count the cost of leading a more or less organized life. It may be a hard road to become a more organized homeschooler. Just remember, you're not journeying alone.

> *Be strong and courageous. Do not be terrified; do not be discouraged, for the* LORD *your God will be with you wherever you go.*
> —JOSHUA 1:9

CHECK IT OFF!

Heart Matters

❑ 1.   I believe that God is a God of order and purpose.

❑ 2.   I choose to become more organized in accordance with God's plan for me.

❑ 3.   I realize that my children and the success of their home-school experience depends upon my level of organization.

❑ 4.   I know that if I want our children to become more organized, they must learn from my example first.

❑ 5.   I am uncomfortable with my current state of organization.

❑ 6.   I desire orderliness just as God does.

2

Why Organize?

To organize or not to organize? Is that really the question? Just the fact that you are reading this shows that on some level you desire orderliness. Homeschooling brings along with it new components to daily life. These components have a tendency to overwhelm and over-run our homes. It's going to take more than a fancy storage closet to maintain order and a sense of peace. It's going to take a change of heart, mind, and action. For some, that means it's going to take a miracle!

"It's just the way I was made," you may argue. I challenge that assertion. You were also just born a sinner, without righteousness of your own, separated from God and sentenced to death. Yet He overcame that lack in your life, didn't He? Contrary to popular belief, "the way I was made" is not too much for God to handle. Do you really think the God of the universe is overwhelmed by your disorganization? Right now you hold the reins and are in control. How is it working for you? Hopefully by the time you're finished with this book you will be willing to let go of your control and let the Holy Spirit direct your path instead.

HEART MATTERS

According to *Vine's Expository Dictionary* (Nashville: Thomas Nelson, 1940), "The *heart*, in its moral significance in the Old

Testament, includes the emotions, the reason and the will." Our choices and actions are the result of the state of our hearts. The two are intricately connected, woven in such a way that one could not exist without the other. Herein lies the problem of disorganization. A disorganized life is a result of the belief that orderliness is neither desirable nor important. Because this problem is so embedded within us, we are tempted to assume that it is impossible to change. But our God is the God of the impossible! For some the heart is easily accessible to God; for others it is protected by a hardened exterior, difficult to penetrate. Difficult but not impossible.

> *"O unbelieving generation," Jesus replied, "how long shall I stay with you? How long shall I put up with you? Bring the boy to me." So they brought him. When the spirit saw Jesus, it immediately threw the boy into a convulsion. He fell to the ground and rolled around, foaming at the mouth. Jesus asked the boy's father, "How long has he been like this?" "From childhood," he answered. "It has often thrown him into fire or water to kill him. But if you can do anything, take pity on us and help us." "'If you can'?" said Jesus. "Everything is possible for him who believes." Immediately the boy's father exclaimed, "I do believe; help me overcome my unbelief!"*
>
> —MARK 9:19-24

This story illustrates a number of truths to those of us who struggle with changing our habits or, deeper still, our heart attitudes.

First, *Jesus sounds slightly exasperated by the unbelief that defines that generation (and ours). Yet He still chooses to heal the boy.* How long does our heavenly Father wait for us to "get it"? He will wait an eternity for His children to wake up and realize the completeness of His power. He waits for you to realize that He has already overcome the world and therefore He can certainly overcome your disorderliness.

Next, *Jesus asks how long the boy has been like this.* "From childhood," the father answers. He'd been this way all his life. There seemed to be no hope of his condition ever changing. Do you feel like that? "I've been this way all my life!" you state unequivocally. The key here is to take the next step and do what the boy's father did: Ask for help from the only One who can give it.

Finally, *the father of the boy asks if Jesus can do anything.* But Jesus turns the table on him and asks back, "'If you can'?" It is up to the father to believe that Jesus is able and thus everything is possible! Do you believe God can do what you ask? It is your unbelief that gets in the way. Pray with a humbleness of heart, "Lord, help my unbelief!" If God can heal a young boy, He can certainly help us be more organized!

What we believe to be true affects what we believe God can do. There are some common beliefs about organization circulating among us. If we believe them, the desire to be organized is suffocated.

• *Organized people are born organized.*

I have a sister who kept her room spotless. She knew where everything was at all times. Everything had a place, and often everything was in its appointed place. My room, on the other hand . . . Well, my solution was to just keep the door closed. I believed that Amy was organized because she was born that way. I also believed that somehow I was missing a gene! Thank God He does not allow us to believe a lie. When I shared a dorm room for the first time in college, I lived with someone messier than myself. And for the first time I was uncomfortable in my space. I decided that I needed to separate myself from her mess; so I began to keep more orderly quarters.

Some of us may be born with a certain disposition to neatness or orderliness. Yet God created us in His image, and that orderly gene is in there. That truth is a great encouragement for the rest of us!

- *The more children you have, the less likely your home is to be organized.*

I know couples who have no children and yet their home is more cluttered than a dollar store. I also know families who home-school eight children and run quite an orderly home. Maybe it's not a matter of how many people live in your home. Maybe it's more a matter of how much stuff each of those individuals have that makes it an organizational nightmare.

Understandably if you homeschool five children, you will be making decisions about five different sets of materials, papers, work spaces, etc. Is the challenge insurmountable? I don't think so. Has God already provided for this contingency? Of course He has. Believe that He has already equipped you to do what He has called you to do. If He expects some orderliness and has blessed you with six children, then He has equipped you to maintain things. Your house may not look like my house. Your storage solutions may not resemble anything I've ever seen. But the desire to become orga-nized is God-given and is not dependent on how many dependents you have!

- *It takes more time than I have to get organized.*

I walk into some people's homes, and it is obvious that they homeschool. The dining room table is covered with papers and projects in progress. The walls function as bulletin boards. Any available floor space is dedicated as the "these books need to be returned to the library" space. I realize that the very thought of try-ing to organize such a space is overwhelming, and I know it will take time. But the time it takes in the beginning will be recouped as you go through your days and weeks maintaining order instead of battling clutter. There are many organizational strategies you may choose to experiment with, but in order for any of them to work in your home, with your family, you must be willing to put in the time it will take to begin anew. Change takes time. Most likely, if you're not willing to make the time, you're really not willing to make the change.

This is similar to making the choice to follow Christ. It takes time to get to know Him. It requires changing how we spend our time. Time spent for ourselves and our own purposes must be changed to time spent in His Word and for His Kingdom. God challenges us with His ways and His Word. It's more a matter of a willing spirit than it is a matter of time.

• *I'm the keeper of the home; therefore, I keep things.*

When we moved across country, we took that opportunity to sort through everything we owned before we ever began packing. At that time the city gave a dumpster free of charge for a week to any resident who asked. We requested a dumpster four weeks in a row and filled it each time! We couldn't believe how much stuff we had held on to. In the beginning it was difficult to throw things away, but quickly it was liberating. It was not uncommon for our neighbors to witness stuff flying out of our attic windows and down into the dumpster below. When we were done, I still felt like we had too much stuff to pack. And I was right, because after a year in our new home there were still twenty boxes left unpacked! Stuff we obviously didn't really need.

Our hearts are like that too. We hold onto old habits and old baggage that maybe served us at one time but are no longer necessary. We hold onto it because we're afraid it won't be there if we need it someday. God's provision for us is complete. Holding onto material possessions, storing up our treasures here on earth, does not provide security. All the things of this world will pass away. There is security in one thing and one thing only—everlasting life!

When we hold onto old habits or old stuff, we are telling God that we don't believe His provision is enough.

• *Highly creative or intelligent people tend to be disorganized.*

The movies commonly portray artisans of all sorts as messy creative folk who live comfortably amongst chaos. Creative genius is also portrayed by a room full of papers or experiments littering every available surface. Although stereotypes have some basis in reality, many artists will argue for order. What if they can't find their materials or supplies? What if they can't account for where their latest work is stored when a buyer comes? What if their genius is overlooked due to distracting clutter? Most creative or intelligent people devise their own system for organizing their thoughts and their products. They have to in order to be recognized for their work.

When our children were very young, we always had paint, clay, paper, markers, crayons, brushes, and containers of all sorts filled with creative delights within arm's reach. They were kept in the lower cabinets for easy access to preschoolers. Many of our friends cringed at the prospect of countertops covered with finger paint and floors littered with Play Doh. Yet with privilege comes responsibility, and we taught our children how to be good stewards of these materials. After all, if an artist does not take care of his tools, his art will suffer. Access with accountability is the key!

Our heavenly Father does not withhold any of His creation from us. From the very beginning we were put in dominion over it for our service, survival, and enjoyment. Yet we are expected to take care of it, no matter how creative we are architecturally or technically. How we plan to use His space and for what purpose are primary considerations. These decisions don't take away from the creativity He has blessed us with—they just focus that creativity. So if you have a budding Picasso, he or she still needs to know how to care for his or her creative environment.

- *Organized people are obsessive.*

Over the years, television sitcoms have poked fun at those who are and aren't organized and orderly. *The Odd Couple* quickly comes to mind. Felix Unger exhibited obsessive/compulsive behavior with regard to keeping order in a home. As much as we made fun of Felix, Oscar's opposite aversion to neatness made us giggle all the more. Meticulous, fastidious, neat-freaks—whatever label you want to assign to naturally organized people is probably not very flattering. Does someone who is highly organized make you feel uncomfortable? If so, the truth is that it isn't the person who is making you feel uncomfortable. It's how what they do sheds light on what you do (or don't do). Have you ever walked into a friend's house and she apologizes profusely about the mess, and yet what you see is spotless? We make ourselves feel better by thinking, *Their home is so sterile,* or *That's a show-house, not a home,* or even *I'd be afraid to get comfortable in that house!* And we'd panic if that same person showed up at our front door unannounced.

There is a point where good stewardship turns into idolatry. If maintaining neatness and order occupies most of your time, money, and worry, then most likely it has become an idol in your life. But the opposite can also be true. If you spend no time in stewardship of your home and your possessions (all gifts from God), then you are disregarding your God-given call to good stewardship. How can we create homeschool environments that are comfortable, yet organized? We must be willing to seek balance.

- *Making lists just reminds me of all I don't get done.*

I remember being very young when I noticed my mother's list. She had one of those grocery shopping list tablets and filled it with not just groceries, but chores she hoped to accomplish, gifts or cards she needed to buy, and appointments that needed to be kept. I don't remember my mom ever sitting me down and telling me that I must make lists. I just did it beginning in junior high school. "To do" lists became a part of my day. I was involved in many activities, and it helped pass the time in school when I finished my work early to make a list of homework and anything else I could think of that I needed to do. At times my lists have become quite exhaustive and intimidating, to say the least. I know I will not accomplish everything on the list, but then I know what I should start with the next day. It helps me organize my thoughts and reflect on my priorities. And boy, does it feel good to check things off that list!

Those who feel that list-making is a defeatist act probably put too much on their list or include things they cannot realistically complete. Lesson plans are lists. Someone once said, "If you don't know where you're going, how will you know when you get there?" A sense of accomplishment goes a long way toward instilling a love for orderliness. Make a list for yourself. Make lists for your children for school. Watch how they are empowered by checking things off their lists.

God has outlined clearly in His Word what He wants us to do while we're here on earth. Without it we would wander aimlessly through this life, accomplishing nothing for His kingdom. The Bible provides a multitude of lists. Lists of genealogies. Lists of rituals. Lists of commandments and expectations. God even has a list of the saints—all who have believed in His Son! A list is a good organizational tool—and man did not create it!

> The heart is deceitful above all things and beyond cure. Who can understand it? I the LORD search the heart and examine the mind, to reward a man according to his conduct, according to what his deeds deserve.
>
> —JEREMIAH 17:9-10

We all need God's honest evaluation of us and His direction for our lives.

MIND MATTERS

Why we do what we do is important. Whether they are misconceptions or just plain lies, what we think wrongly can sabotage our efforts to get organized. Learning how to discern the truth when you hear it will help combat faulty thinking. Practice sifting your thoughts and opinions through God's Word. Only then can you correct mistaken thinking. Surround yourself with godly counsel, and "lean not on your own understanding" (Proverbs 3:5).

"I am what I am, and that's all that I am." Popeye the Sailor couldn't have been more wrong. For those operating without the power of the Holy Spirit, this saying is justifiable. But we who know Jesus Christ have that power, and with God's help we can change how we think. For many of us, how we think is more of a habit and less of an intentional pursuit. We are on autopilot most of the time. Doing things the way we've always done them. Thinking the way we've always thought. But old habits can be broken and replaced with new ones. Below are some ways we can break out of bad habits of the mind. Teach your children to do likewise, and orderly thinking will become your greatest tool.

Learning to Discern

One of the greatest gifts we have is the gift of the Holy Spirit. Because of this precious gift, we are now able to understand the Scriptures and to know the truth when we hear it. Yet this is not a mystical occurrence, but a gradual process of growing up and growing in the Word of God. There is joy in discovery! I'm not here to tell you step by step how to get organized. My desire for you is to discover for yourself what it means to live an orderly life according to biblical principles. God leads us all differently. The Holy Spirit will work in your life differently than He works in mine.

The desire to know Him better will be honored. Ask and it will be given to you, in accordance with His will (Matthew 7:7). Start by learning how to study the Bible. If you've never been part of a group that teaches a method of study, find one! If you have, dig out those old notes and refresh your memory. Finding out what God has to say about living an orderly life will not just fall into your lap. You must become a seeker of wisdom. The most successful seekers follow a search pattern. Therein lies organization!

Creative Thinking

How we do something is a choice we all make on a daily basis. There is more than one way to do most anything. Unfortunately, many of us are stuck in the "one size fits all" mode of thinking. If one way didn't work, we throw our hands up in defeat and say, "That didn't work; so all is lost!" And then we don't try another method. Believe it or not, God has blessed us each with a creative mind. After all, we were made in His image, and you must admit God is quite creative.

Creative thinking is a new habit of mind. Practically, there are a number of ways we can exercise our creativity when it comes to thinking. Fluency, versatility, and originality are three of these ways. *Fluency* refers to generating as many ideas as possible, not unlike brainstorming. *Versatility* refers to generating as many *different* kinds of ideas as possible. *Originality* refers to generating ideas no one else has thought of (not easy to do, but worth the pursuit). For example, let's try this exercise:

How many ways can you think of to store your children's schoolwork?

First, let me share some rules about brainstorming. The term means to generate ideas, but often we censor our ideas before we verbalize them. We reject them too quickly. Just write down whatever comes into your mind without judging the idea. Just get it down! Later you can evaluate those ideas, but for now the goal is to generate them.

Think of as many ideas as possible. Now look at your ideas and be flexible. Do some of the ideas lead naturally to others? Can they be modified slightly to come up with additional possibilities?

Finally, can you think of at least one thing that you've never heard anyone else doing to solve this problem? It may be silly or outrageous, and yet it may be a possible solution. The idea is to let the ideas flow, no matter how ridiculous they may seem.

The amount of ideas can easily double if you do this exercise with someone else. Our children sometimes come up with the most original ideas. They haven't yet learned to censor their ideas like we adults have. See what ideas you can come up with together.

Problem Solving

Approaching problems with logic is a new concept to some. We daily face dilemmas and problems with regard to homeschooling. Some might be big, others seemingly insignificant. Many of us rush headlong into problem solving and end up on an emotional roller coaster. An organized approach to problem solving will do two things. It will take the emotion out of the mess of the problem and will offer credible solutions.

For example, what if your daughter is really struggling with reading and she's eight years old. You've homeschooled her from the very start, and you watch helplessly as she wrestles with letters and their sounds. She hates reading and feels like she's being punished every time you make her do it. What can you do? Everyone reading this is now thinking of how they would handle this situation or have handled it themselves in the past. But you are reading this alone and can't hear others' solutions. So what should you do? There is a simple yet logical process that can help. You'll have to use your brainstorming skills from the previous exercise. There are basically five steps to solving problems:

- Step 1: *Pinpoint the actual problem.* Try to verbalize the problem at the end of this sentence, "In what ways might I . . . ?" Do that and you've taken the emotion out of the dilemma and made what at first seemed messy easy to identify.

• Step 2: *Fact finding.* What other information will you need to solve this problem? Do you have to consult with experts, research online or in books, or talk to your daughter? Gather as much information about the problem as possible. This is probably the longest part of this process, but it is also the most valuable.

• Step 3: *Idea finding.* Now use those brainstorming skills and generate ideas for solutions. Remember, don't censor or judge them. Just get them down!

• Step 4: *Solution finding.* Look at your list of ideas for solutions, and choose the ones you believe are most feasible. Now is the time to judge them. You must choose one based upon what you value. Does it take time? Does it take money? Will it mean a change of environment? Is it biblical? Will it disrupt the rest of the family? What will it do to the stress level in your home? Come up with your own list of criteria from which to judge your feasible solutions. Once you've done this, one solution will jump out at you as being the logical choice. And sometimes it might not have been your first choice under different circumstances.

• Step 5: *Action plan.* Now it's time to put that chosen solution into action. How will you do that? What steps do you need to take in order to make that solution a reality? With that in mind, all that's left is to actually put it into motion.

Ideally, your chosen solution is the best solution, but sometimes it doesn't turn out that way. What was number 2 on your list? Maybe it is really the better choice. Only you will know.

Try this process on a problem that isn't as emotionally charged as your daughter not reading well. Let's go back to the question from our first exercise and rephrase it:

In what ways might I store my children's schoolwork?

Try this five-step process on this problem and see what you come up with!

Priority Setting

How we choose to spend our time reveals our priorities. The problem comes when we don't take time to think about how we spend our time. Even as homeschoolers, we can find ourselves running here and there to such an extent that the immediate needs of our family and home fall by the wayside. Have you ever taken the time to list your priorities on paper? If not, maybe it's time to do so. An easy way to find out how you're spending your time is by writing down everything, and I mean *everything*, you do over the course of a week. It is just like when you are learning how to create a budget; the first thing you're asked to do is write down and account for every penny spent during the month. It's also like starting a diet and writing down everything you eat over the course of one week. It helps to see the whole picture in black and white.

Now it is a matter of categorizing how your time is spent, just like putting things in categories for a budget or food groups for a diet. Here are my categories; yours may vary, of course:

- Time with and for family.
- Time with and for God (and His kingdom).
- Time with and for friends.
- Time with and for extended family.
- Time with and for myself.
- Time for my home.

The idea here is to see where things fall within these categories. Do you notice some that are fuller than others? Do you notice one that is empty? If you were to set these categories according to God's priorities, which would come first? Homeschooling falls under both *Time with and for family* and *Time with and for God*. You are training your children in the ways they should go, and those ways are God's ways! Is this the priority that you thought it was in your family? Or have you taken it for granted that it will be taken care of in the long run? God deserves our first thoughts, our first offerings, and not our leftovers.

This can be quite a humbling experience, but that's when you know you're doing it right! We are called to be humble in His sight. Let Him humble you today!

BODY MATTERS

At this point you have investigated what you believe and have examined your thoughts and ways of thinking. Whatever action you take next is almost an involuntary action. It is the natural consequence to what has come before. What you do with what you've learned thus far is up to you, but now your heart has been pricked, and the Holy Spirit is tugging on you to follow. Will you follow?

CHECK IT OFF!

Heart Matters

❏   1.   I believe that my disorderliness is not too big for God.

❏   2.   I am willing to let go of my control and let the Holy Spirit direct my path instead.

❏   3.   I know it's important for me to model the same habits I expect from my children.

Mind Matters

❏   4.   I am willing to think about why I do what I do.

❑ 5. I am willing to approach problems with more logic and less emotion.

❑ 6. I realize in order to make this change, I must be willing to change my priorities.

Body Matters

❑ 7. I am willing to step in faith toward a more orderly life. God has already equipped me.

3

Organize Your Thoughts

Remember that saying quoted in the last chapter, "If you don't know where you're going, how will you know when you get there?" Let's rephrase it in its opposite connotation: "If you know where you're going, you'll know when you get there." It is no longer a question, but a statement of fact. This chapter deals strictly with the facts.

There are different approaches to homeschooling. There are unschoolers, traditional schoolers, eclectic homeschoolers, and more. Whether I am conducting a workshop or hosting a homeschool chat room, these approaches inevitably butt heads. It is not my intention to say one way is better than the other. But I do suggest that being organized is a welcome characteristic for any approach to homeschooling.

One of the foundational issues surrounding organized thought as it applies to homeschooling is the issue of choosing a destination. Do you know where you're going? Every journey has a final destination. Some of us meander on our way and check out every scenic overlook, while others prefer to follow the designated route. There may be side trips, but they are planned. This chapter speaks to those who prefer to use some sort of map. Take time during your reading of this chapter to consider where you want to go and how you intend to get there.

GOAL-SETTING

This term, for some, brings to mind corporate images of stiff-necked executives in boardrooms and long documents outlining five-, ten-, and twenty-year plans. Those who are naturally goal-oriented welcome a discussion of goal-setting, but for others it is unsettling. Keep in mind throughout this book that the idea is to raise your awareness of organization and to encourage you to dig deeper for yourself as to what areas in your homeschool life need more order. Let's first discuss the essential elements of goal-setting:

Who? Should everyone set goals? I don't know about everyone—I only know about myself and my children. Without goals our journey would just be aimless wandering from experience to experience, and I'm not sure what that would realistically prepare my children for in life. Goal-setting is for you if you want to feel like you and your children actually accomplished something during your homeschool experience, whether it lasted one year or ran the duration of the school years.

What? What do goals look like? Are there different types? Goals should be attainable. Dreams may not be, but goals certainly should be. Here are some synonyms for *goal*:

- aim
- ambition
- bull's-eye
- calling
- design
- destination
- end

- intention
- mark
- mission
- objective
- plan
- purpose
- target

All of these synonyms are purposeful words that denote that a plan of some kind is in place. Does God have a plan? He has many plans. Some include us as individuals, and some include His entire kingdom. As you study the Bible, you can see His plan expertly outlined. It is not haphazard.

And we know that in all things God works for the good of those
who love him, who have been called according to his purpose.
—ROMANS 8:28

There is a plan—a purpose. And *all* things, not just some
things, work toward His purpose.

When? If you have never purposefully planned at least some
aspect of your children's education, now is the time. Time is probably our most precious commodity, and it is dwindling down
moment by moment. Christ may return tonight! Personally, I
hope to be able to stand before Him unashamed. We are called to
redeem the time, "making the most of every opportunity"
(Ephesians 5:16). When should we sit down with our children to
design these goals? Prior to the beginning of the school year is
best. However, if you are reading this in the middle of the year,
today is the day!

Where? Should these goal-setting sessions be formal? Not necessarily. Can we just sit on the couch and talk about them? Of
course. But I encourage you to take them seriously, so your children will take them seriously. I take my children out for breakfast
before we start school for the year, and we talk about goals over a
bagel. And yes, we write them down. Putting something in writing
does two things. It tells people you're serious. It also makes it easier to refer to later. Then periodically throughout the year we go out
for bagels again and talk about where we are with respect to those
goals. It's sort of a conference with cream cheese! God had His goals
written down for our referral, and because of that we certainly
know He is serious about them.

How? Goal-setting is a relatively simple process. You can make
it as complex as you want, but remember that if your expectations
are unrealistic, your disappointment will be great. You want your
children to experience success; so start small. You can always, and

should, raise the bar later. Think about the ways in which your child works. With what does he or she have difficulty? Is his work neat enough? Does she finish on time regularly? Are his materials organized? Does she always complete her tasks? If not, this is a good place to start. Goals for academics are a given. We all want our children to complete fifth grade math; so we don't really need to write that down. What we do need to encourage are strong work habits, consistent self-initiative, and quality work. This is where goal-setting has the potential to change habits and hearts.

CREATING CONNECTIONS

Everything we do within our homeschools should lead to the goals we have set with our children. It is so easy to get distracted and get off track. You might receive a homeschool support group newsletter outlining all the field trips they have planned for the year, and you sign up for many of them. There's nothing wrong with going on field trips or engaging in activities on the spur of the moment. But I caution you not to make a habit of it. The more time we spend away from home, the less time we have to work on the business at hand. I strongly recommend that all, or as many as possible, activities relate to attaining the goals you have set forth.

I am so grateful for the model God provides. We know that if we are to walk within His will for us, we must be mindful of our choices and how we spend our time. The same can be said for walking along our homeschool journey. Think before you act, and monitor how time is spent.

Below is a process that can help you stay on track:

• *Ready!* (*Choose Your Goal.*) Before you go shopping at the homeschool convention or order from one of the hundreds of homeschool catalogs, have your goals in mind (better yet, have them on paper). The goal is the target; the curricula are the arrows. We must have a target, or why bother with arrows?

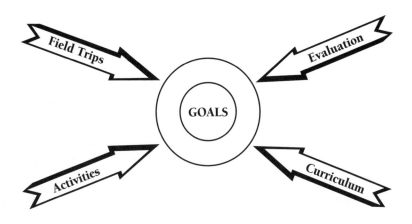

• *Aim! (Choose Your Curriculum.)* Matching curriculum choices to goals is just a matter of staying focused when you shop. If you don't, it's like going to the grocery store when you're hungry. You spend too much and buy things you don't really need. Going shopping with a list in hand is always more efficient. Make a list of curriculum choices that will help you meet your goals with your children. Then if you buy extra items, you'll know they are just for fun. Staying focused on the goal when you shop also keeps costs down. Since most home-schoolers have limited resources, this is good stewardship with God's money.

• *Fire! (Engage in Activities.)* If you aren't careful in your buying, you will have a lot of interesting stuff to choose from— probably more than you need. It is important to choose carefully what learning activities you will use to reach your goals. If not, you will not hit that target. This also applies to field trips and additional experiences that come your way. Just because your support group is going on a field trip to a bakery to see how bread is made doesn't mean you have to. Unless, of course, you are studying something along those lines. You must strike a balance between activities that are interesting just because they're interesting and interesting activities that help you meet your goals. It's also a matter of efficient use of time. How many arrows do you want to waste before hitting your target?

• *Score? (Evaluate Success.)* Some of what we choose to do with our children is right on, and some of it is just in the right neighborhood. Collectively, what is your score? If the majority of what you do doesn't hit or come close to the bull's-eye, the score will be low. If most of what you do comes close with a few bull's-eyes, you can safely say you've met your goals.

Some people think that being so calculating takes all the fun out of learning. I disagree. Actually I have found that the love of learning increases when it is focused. That's when everything clicks! It's like when a batter hits the ball right in the sweet spot. I love teaching in the sweet spot!

ARE LESSON PLANS PART OF THE PLAN?

Lesson plans in some way, shape, or form are recommended. They may exist as checklists for our children, formal "write in the little box" lesson plans for you, or even a note explaining what our children should hope to accomplish in a given time. Yes, write it down. Yes, be specific. Remember that writing it down shows that we're serious, and it gives us all something to which we can refer later.

Whatever way you choose to write lesson plans, remember that it helps you maintain a focus on the task at hand. Depending upon our memory is foolish for most of us. If you have come this far and have chosen goals, matched curriculum, and engaged in worthwhile activities, why wouldn't you document how you spend your time? Keep in mind that lesson plans are not written in stone. They can be amended at any time. At the end of a week you will know how close your child got to his target and how much farther he has yet to go.

REFLECTIONS

When you reflect on something, you consider it, contemplate it, speculate on it, or deliberate about it. Reflection is powerful and intentional! So often *what* we do is questioned because we didn't consider *why* we do what we do. When you take the time necessary to reflect on the whys, it brings what you're doing back into focus. Sometimes we get off target. Sometimes we get lazy and don't aim properly. For whatever reason, we've let things slip and the level of learning drops.

So what should we reflect on? How should we conduct this reflection? How often should we reflect? The answers to these questions will vary from person to person. The bottom line is to reflect, but I can offer you some suggestions to get you started. This is not the time to evaluate your child's success. It is the time to evaluate your own as a parent-educator. It's *your* reflection; so get ready to look in the mirror!

• *Keep a journal.* Many people cringe at the prospect of doing this. Just the thought of it somehow conjures up images of a dreaded writing assignment during their school days. A journal must have a purpose, and when it does it writes itself. I keep a three-ring binder with lesson plans, support group newsletters, correspondence with the state, and a section devoted to my journal. I write in it when I think of it. Even now, at the beginning of our school year, I can go back and see what concerned me, what made me laugh, what milestones my children reached, and even what doubts I might have had. When

I look back over the last three years of homeschooling, I notice that most of my concerns change from year to year. One, the insatiable learning appetite of our oldest son, tends to recur. You might write in your journal every day; you might write in it once a month. Just write in it.

• *Make goals for yourself as an educator.* Goal-setting isn't just for your children; it's for you as well. It's important that children see us do the very thing we expect of them. As you begin to think about what goals you will set for yourself as a teacher, consider your attitude, your habits, and your own spiritual growth. Do you need to be more patient? More attentive? Less insistent? A better listener? More consistent? Less intimidating? All traits that you believe will lead to harmony in your homeschool deserve attention. As you write them down, it will be easier to focus on them. Then find ways to meet those goals. Do you need to join a Bible study? Stay home more? Get more sleep? Get less sleep? Learn a new skill? The effort to set and meet your own goals will go far in improving the quality of the homeschool experience for your children and yourself.

• *Be willing to put the blame on yourself when things go wrong.* There are two extreme reactions when our children are not learning as expected. On one extreme, the teacher blames herself entirely for the failing of her student. On the other extreme, the teacher takes no blame, believing that it is up to the student to learn what has been provided. Both are wrong. As homeschoolers we desire our children to become independent learners, and sometimes we back off too soon. Over and over again I have heard parents say, "Yes, he's still having trouble with writing, but he'll figure it out eventually on his own." This is not necessarily so. If he is given the right instruction and encouragement, he will learn. But if you have never worked on a skill and leave him to develop it on his own, he may never get it. There is a balance between leading your child by the hand through his education and leaving him to wander aimlessly on his own. *You* must create that balance.

• *Become an active learner.* It's very easy to fall into a passive routine as a home educator. Our children may be working really hard, but we can sometimes get lax about the learning process. As children mature and become more independent (our goal for them), we tend to back off. Believe it or not, this is not the time to leave them out there on their own. They are learning more complex skills and concepts that require our feedback. This is the time when they must move from competence (just doing the bare minimum) to quality (polished efforts, more than expected). We don't improve without feedback. Some parents take an active role in the learning process and may even take a class at their local junior college with their teenager, both to learn it for themselves and to be the resource their child needs. If we become complacent, there is danger our children will become complacent as well.

Action minus thought is ineffective and sometimes foolish. Planning, goal-setting, and keeping a journal of self-reflection are all ways we can think before we act.

A simple man believes anything, but a prudent man gives thought to his steps.

—Proverbs 14:15

If we are to walk in wisdom, we must consider *why* we do what we do. We desire that our children will grow to be wise, and wisdom is thoughtful. Making decisions, making choices, and solving problems all require wisdom and thoughtful consideration. We are given opportunity after opportunity to hone our thinking during our homeschool experience. Let us not allow it to go to waste.

CHECK IT OFF!

Heart Matters

❑ 1. I will take the time to decide where we're going by setting goals.

❑ 2. I believe it is just as important to set goals for myself as for my children.

Mind Matters

❑ 3. I will choose activities that help us reach our goals.

❑ 4. I will consider the impact that time away from home has on our homeschool efforts.

Body Matters

❑ 5. In some way, shape, or form I will plan for my children.

❑ 6. I will spend time reflecting on what is working and what is not and why.

4

Organize Your Time

Before we brought our children home to school, I went back to work. I thought it was the right *time*. What I found out was that it was not God's *timing*, and my family paid the price for a year as I worked until the end of my contract. How did I know it wasn't God's timing? First of all, I had no peace. Second, going back to teaching lost its appeal almost immediately as I realized that after being at home with my children for five years, I was now accountable to countless others for how I spent my time. I felt trapped, confined. I felt like my life was slipping away from me at light speed! God's timing is perfect, but when we make choices of how to spend the time He's provided according to our own desires, we often experience frustration, doubt, and undue stress.

Many of us never seem to find enough time to do what we need to do. Others of us seem to have time on our hands. Yet somehow we all seem to find the time to do the things we *want* to do. Again it is a matter of balance. Finding that balance is not only necessary for homeschooling—it is necessary in order to please God. The Bible has much to say about time and how we spend it. I've learned there is precious little of it! Our children watch how we spend our time. They in turn will make their own choices regarding how to spend their time. What do we want them to learn from us?

TO SCHEDULE OR NOT TO SCHEDULE?

As homeschoolers we do not jump when the bell rings or adhere to strict school-day schedules with fifty-minute class periods. Yet in many states homeschoolers are expected to follow specific guidelines with regard to time. For example, here in Colorado the district in which we homeschool requires that we spend four hours of instruction per day for 172 days per school year. When the school year begins and ends is not specified. Other states have similar regulations. Check your own state for guidelines. However, the district does not dictate how we schedule those four hours per day.

The issue of scheduling is a hot one among homeschoolers. Below is a list of common complaints some homeschoolers make when confronted with the topic of scheduling:

• I don't keep track of how long we do school. It's not necessary.

• I don't want the state dictating what we do in our homeschool!

• I don't want my children to have to submit to the demands of a schedule.

• My children make their own schedules!

These and other statements reveal a variety of heart issues. Usually given in response to another homeschooler who desires to maintain some kind of schedule, these comments can be received as defensive and intimidating. If any of these statements or others like them describe your reaction to the word *schedule*, I suggest you prayerfully consider your motives for saying them. What do we believe to be true about how we spend our time? Remember, what we believe to be true becomes what we think, and what we think becomes what we do.

With regard to which approach—scheduling or no scheduling—is better for students, there are arguments for and against both. Some consider strict schedules to be stifling and confining, turning learners into academic robots. Others consider no scheduling to invite chaos and a lack of focus for the learner. Either, taken to the extreme, can be detrimental. Again, our goal is to create a comfortable balance in our homes. As a former teacher I thought I would be a strictly scheduled homeschooler. However, I have found that we are all much more comfortable and motivated when following a more relaxed schedule. Flexibility is the key. Sickness, character development issues, home businesses, and even fatigue all mess with a strict schedule. The beauty of homeschooling is that we can make decisions based on the needs of our own family and not just follow someone else's rules.

TIME WELL SPENT

How do we know if our time has been well spent? If we finish the things we hoped to get done, it is time well spent. If we don't accomplish what we hoped to get done, somehow we think our time was wasted. But what if you hoped to complete Sam's math lesson within an hour but instead spent that time searching for Bible references about *pride* after Sam boasted to his siblings that he was gifted in math? Was that a waste of time? The math did not get done. Yet in God's eyes the time was spent in a productive manner. He provided an opportunity for Sam to learn more about himself and about God. That was definitely time well spent. It is important that we are flexible enough in our scheduling to allow for godly interruptions.

To Whom Are We Accountable for Our Time?

Below you will find a list of people to whom I am accountable for my time with regard to homeschooling. Your list will vary in length depending upon how involved you and your family are in outside activities:

 • the district office (to turn in my paperwork on time)

- my children
- my husband
- the moms in our church homeschool support group (even though I'm the leader)
- the homeschoolers who participate in the online chats I host weekly
- the teachers at the homeschool enrichment classes our children attend weekly
- the homeschoolers who e-mail me with questions
- the homeschoolers I meet at homeschool conventions when I speak
- God

Whether my list seems short or overwhelmingly long to you, one person stands out as the key to it all. When I'm willing to be accountable to God for how I spend my time, all the others to whom I am accountable will be satisfied. Trying to please everyone else on that list before God only results in frustration and failure.

How do we become accountable before God about how we spend our time? First, we must humble ourselves and admit that we are not able to fulfill all the demands on our time by ourselves. Second, we must strive to know better what God Himself thinks about how time should be spent. Third, we must act in a way that shows that we think as God thinks. The only way to do this effectively is by spending more time in prayer. *Show me how to spend my time, Lord.*

Deadlines, Timelines, and Time Clocks

What are we to do with those deadlines that we've either imposed upon ourselves or that have been imposed upon us? Strive to submit to them! And teach your children how to submit to them. If the goal is to be on time, try to finish early. If you have yet to impose deadlines on your children's work, it is never too late to start. Time management skills are required in every job description. This is not something children magically figure out on their own. It is something we must teach them, and we have only a precious few years in which to do it!

TO EVERYTHING THERE IS A SEASON

During a particularly frustrating time in my life, I was involved in too many things and became completely overwhelmed. I was reminded gently of this truth: *God willing, there's time to do it all— just not all at the same time.* Many homeschool parents have the SuperMom or SuperDad complex. We believe we can do it all. Unfortunately, we forget to count the cost before running off to save the world. If we're too busy to consider the consequences of how we spend our time, then we're too busy.

There's a time to be busy, and there's a time to be still. Being still is required *before* being busy. "Be still, and know that I am God" (Psalm 46:10). Without the stillness, we don't know how to be busy, when or where to be busy, or with what to be busy. When we're not still, we can't hear God or know His will. When we're too busy, we're about our own business and not His.

What did King Solomon say? The book of Ecclesiastes examines the issue of what we value and how we spend our time here on this earth. Solomon, renowned for his wisdom, considered every aspect of human life and priorities by comparing them to every aspect of God and His priorities. There was no comparison. His conclusion? All is vanity! Everything we do, no matter how noble the cause, if it isn't to please God, is done to please ourselves. There is no in-between. Even the decision to homeschool is vanity if it doesn't please God. It may be noble, it may be the right thing to do for our children, but it may also be only to please ourselves. If your day is full of "everything under the sun" and you're burnt out, then maybe you're being offered a gentle reminder that there is a time for everything, just not everything at one time.

What is there time for?

> There is a time for everything,
> and a season for every activity under heaven:
> a time to be born and a time to die,
> a time to plant and a time to uproot,
> a time to kill and a time to heal,
> a time to tear down and a time to build,
> a time to weep and a time to laugh,
> a time to mourn and a time to dance,
> a time to scatter stones and a time to gather them,
> a time to embrace and a time to refrain,
> a time to search and a time to give up,
> a time to keep and a time to throw away,
> a time to tear and a time to mend,
> a time to be silent and a time to speak,
> a time to love and a time to hate,
> a time for war and a time for peace.
>
> ECCLESIASTES 3:1-8

As we reflect upon all that King Solomon considered, we see there is nothing new under the sun. The struggle with how people spend their time has been going on from the beginning. So even if you vow to spend your time more wisely, according to God's purposes, you will struggle with that vow if you made that vow by your own power. On the days when we spend our time doing school in a more purposeful fashion, it is satisfying and brings peace. On other days, when we flit from activity to activity as if powered by the wind, it is disappointing and brings agitation.

Is there time for field trips and experiments and going down rabbit trails while we homeschool? Of course there is; just not necessarily all at the same time. There is a time to go on field trips, and there is a time to stay at home. There is a time to do hands-on experiments, and there is a time to work from the book. There is a time to investigate side topics, and there is a time to stick to the curriculum. There is a time to be flexible, and there is a time to remain rigid. The idea is to remember whose time it is that we are utilizing. It certainly isn't our own.

TIME TROUBLES

I have yet to meet a person who was content with how he or she manages his or her time. Most of us think we have too little time to do too many things. The television commercials showing the harried working mom who doesn't have time to prepare dinner or the career-minded dad who spends most of his life flying from one business trip to the next are real life for most people. Homeschoolers are no different. Just because you teach your children at home doesn't mean you sit around the rest of the day eating bonbons and watching the afternoon talk shows.

If you homeschool and keep a clean house, does that mean you must have too much time on your hands? We are quick to judge one another about how we spend our time. If you homeschool and much of the schoolwork gets done in the car in between errands, I might raise an eyebrow. Conversely, if you homeschool and say you are always done before noon, I also might raise an eyebrow. But raising an eyebrow and opening my mouth are two different things. It's difficult enough to manage my own homeschool, let alone try to manage yours!

Our quest—this bears repeating—is to create balance. What follows are the extremes on the scale. Think of your own homeschool day, and see where you can add or subtract to gain a semblance of balance.

Not Enough Time

Some people are more sensitive than others to their own level of tolerance when it comes to getting too busy. Others, like myself, don't see it until it's too late. We're in too deep, with too many responsibilities, to manage successfully. If we don't learn how to say no, how will our children learn to do so? What are some of the telltale signs of being too busy?

- I have difficulty sleeping (a symptom of stress).
- I frequently feel under some sort of deadline.
- I don't enjoy schooltime with my children.
- I often feel as if we don't get enough done.
- I often sacrifice care of the home in favor of time with my children.
- I say yes without thinking when anyone asks for my help.
- I rarely cook.
- I'm considering putting my children into school because I'm overwhelmed.

There are many more indicators of *too busy* people, but these are some of the most common. Granted, certain personalities tend to gravitate toward a busier lifestyle; but if it is at the expense of your child's homeschooling, then how you spend your time must be considered. Some of us become too busy because deep down we're trying to justify our choice to homeschool. If we seem busy, then we must be productive. But sometimes busy is just busy.

Too Much Time

Do some people actually have too much time on their hands? I know it's hard to believe, but it's true. How can you tell if you have too much time on your hands? Consider the following:

- I watch in excess of two hours of television *every* day.
- I visit an online chat room or am on the Internet more than two hours per day.

• I don't feel motivated to volunteer or serve in a ministry at this time.

• I read at least five or six books per month.

I'm sure there are many other characteristics of people who have too much time on their hands. Again, personality does play a part in how we spend our time. But God created us, and if He has work for us to do, then He has also equipped us to do that work. We worry about our children who watch too much television or play too many video games because (1) they're not getting enough exercise, (2) they're not engaging socially with those around them, and (3) they're becoming lazy. As adults we should be concerned about those same issues for ourselves. I won't say that if you have a clean house you must have too much time on your hands. But I will say that if you know what the topic has been on every afternoon talk show that day, you are not using your time wisely.

Let's Play "Beat the Clock"

How can we manage our time more efficiently and in a way that pleases God? Do we need better Day-Timers® or electronic organizers? Do we need a housekeeper or a lawn service or a spouse who takes more of the responsibility? Do we need to enroll our children in school part-time? Yes and no. All of our schedules could use some adjustment. Even when you think you have everything under control, the law of entropy is in place. Everything breaks down. Everything is in a state of decay. That perfect homeschool day is bound to fall apart.

The answer is not to be a clock-watcher. The answer is to be a God-watcher. Keep yourself focused on how and when He wants you to do what you do, and your adjustments will be minor. Here on Earth it is impossible to keep perfect time. Whether your homeschool clock is too fast or too slow, it is better to leave it in the hands of the Master Timekeeper.

JUST IN TIME

Why does it matter how we spend our time? You may be intending to homeschool for the duration of your children's school years and think that it will all work out in the end. Or this may be your first and only homeschool year, and you are consumed with the time factor. Either way, as a Christian you are in command of the time given to you. Time should not rule you. Why does this matter?

> Be very careful, then, how you live—not as unwise but as wise, making the most of every opportunity, because the days are evil.
>
> —EPHESIANS 5:15-16

Investigate the following:
• How do the unwise live?
• How do the wise live?
• How are the days evil?
Only then can you make "the most of every opportunity."

CHECK IT OFF!

Heart Matters

❑   1.   I know I need to focus on God's timing and not my own.

❑   2.   I know that how I spend my time reflects my priorities.

Mind Matters

❑   3.   Children function better within certain limitations, with schedules.

❑ 4. Given the diversity of distractions, a flexible schedule works best for homeschoolers.

Body Matters

❑ 5. I will create a schedule that takes our family's needs into consideration.

❑ 6. I will say, "Let me think about it and get back to you" when someone asks me to do something.

Organize Your Space

It seems we never have enough space. The comedian George Carlin is famous for his "I need a place for my stuff!" routine. He made fun of the fact that we all have way too much stuff. Whether you live in a two-bedroom apartment or a 5,000-square-foot custom-built home, chances are you believe homeschooling takes up too much space in your home.

On the other hand, there are many who do not have a designated school area—by choice. School is a part of life and therefore a part of the home. This chapter is designed to help homeschoolers who desire to bring a sense of order to the space they already have. How we organize our space depends on a variety of factors. There are specific design considerations that can help to make it all work together. Whether we have too little or too much, space should serve our needs, not the other way around.

SPACE CONSIDERATIONS

Most of us would agree that we need more space. But unless you are in the market for a bigger house or have a remodeling budget, you're going to have to make do with what you have. The first aspect of space planning is to assess your current situation. Taking an inventory of how the current spaces are being used is usually an eye-opener.

Room by Room

With a pad of paper in hand, take a tour of your home. As you enter each room, write down how it is currently being used—its function. Then write down the answers to the following:

- Is this use temporary or permanent?
- Is it being used for its original function?
- Is it important to me that this room retain its current function?

After touring your home, your list may look something like this for a particular room.

DINING ROOM

Function: schoolroom

1. Temporary
2. Not original function
3. Desire it to be a dining room again.

You will be tempted to make decisions about these spaces, but I encourage you to wait. As you assess each space in your home, you will find that you can already see possibilities. There's power in observation.

Public or Private

No, we're not talking about choice of schools. It's important to recognize whether you are more of a *private* or a *public* person. Why does this matter? It matters because it helps you make decisions about your space. If you are more public, then you don't mind if school is conducted in the middle of the living room. If you are more private, you will probably choose a more secluded area for school. The following questions may help you decide, if it isn't already obvious to you:

- I have caller ID and don't answer the phone if I don't have to. (Private)

- I prefer to complete the day's schooling before we either go out or have someone over. (Private)
- We entertain guests on a regular basis. (Public)
- I welcome distractions! (Public)
- If other children want to play, I prefer they play at our house. (Public)
- I prefer my visitors to call before they come. (Private)

If all of these questions apply to you, then you are probably a very flexible person who does not have a public or private preference. Some of you will find you are one way or the other. The idea is to recognize any preferences.

Frank Lloyd Wright, the renowned architect, had very strong opinions about public versus private with regard to the home. He designed his spaces with the following beliefs in mind:

- The house shelters the family not only from nature, but from the world itself.
- The front door should not be an open invitation to anyone just walking by.
- Usually a house should turn its back to the street.
- Once you walk into a home, it should be warm, inviting, and comfortable.
- There should be an obvious transition from public to private spaces in a home.
- Rooms and uses should flow naturally throughout the home.
- Rooms for children should not be adjacent to public spaces.

The playroom in Wright's own home in Oak Park, Illinois, where his children not only played but probably did most of their learning, was tucked behind the main living quarters, yet close to the bedrooms.

Wright's approach to establishing public and private spaces

may seem extreme and even antisocial, but his emphasis was on the family, not on those who only visited the home. As we consider spaces for our children and homeschooling, it is necessary that we address our own need for privacy. It's your home and your family. They are the only ones you need to please.

Needs of Individuals

How we organize our space is dependent in part on the needs of the individuals who live within that space. If you work from home, then you will have a place for a desk and/or computer. If you enjoy crafts, you might have a space dedicated to that activity. Sometimes the activity chooses a space, and sometimes personality or personal preference chooses it. For example, our oldest son has difficulty concentrating and is easily distracted. When he is doing school-work, he sits in an adjacent room away from his brother, my chores, and his Legos. But he's still within sight in case he needs my assistance. It's a priority to provide for his need for little to no distraction.

Some families have home businesses, and school must be conducted close to the phone or other business-associated equipment. Other children are not yet able to work independently and require constant supervision. Young children require space to spread out or need to sit on the floor to do their work. Whatever your child's particular needs, those needs must be incorporated into the design of your home and school environment.

Relationships

Another important consideration with regard to space planning is the relationships that interrelate within the space. How much hands-on time do your children require of you during school? How much supervision? Are older children instrumental in the teaching of the younger? Does your high school son work better when you're not around? Does your seventh grade daughter prefer to work away from her siblings? Are there strained relationships that require time and space for healing? Or is the cohesiveness of your family its greatest strength? Whatever the relationship, consider its impact when choosing how to organize your space.

Configuring an optimum work and living space can be quite satisfying when the above factors are taken into consideration. It's not just a matter of furniture placement—it's a matter of design.

YOUR WISH LIST

Those of us who feel space-deprived also feel trapped by the space we have. We mistakenly believe there is no other way to arrange things. I now give you permission to dream. Consider the following questions. What would you do if you could wave a magic wand over your home? In a perfect world, how would the space function? If you had an unlimited budget, what would you change? Admittedly, many of your answers may not become reality, but they indicate what is important to you about how your space functions. That's important to know.

For example, a wish list might look something like this:

1. My ideal home would have a school area close to the kitchen, yet private enough that we are not disturbed by the front door.

2. My ideal home would have a library area close to the school area.

3. My ideal home would have a dedicated room for school with a door that I can close.

4. My ideal home would have the computer area as part of the school area.

Make your wish list and allow yourself to dream!

IDEAS

Most likely your own list describing the details of your ideal space was limited—limited by your own imagination. We are our own worst critics. We judge our ideas as inadequate, unrealistic, and even stupid. So instead we come up with ideas that are acceptable, credible, and safe. Yet as you consider how to design your home and school spaces, allow yourself the freedom to think outside the box. The solution that really works might just be the one that was rejected early on because it seemed so unusual.

Brainstorming is the most effective way to generate as many ideas or solutions as possible. Most people who say they've tried brainstorming and found it didn't work probably didn't do it properly. There are rules that must be followed in order for it to be effective. Start by asking an idea-seeking question.

• What are all the ways I can incorporate school within our common space?

• What are all the ways I can seclude our school space?

Consider the four rules of brainstorming:

1. *Quantity is wanted*: The goal is to generate as many ideas as possible.

2. *Free-wheeling is necessary*: Allow yourself to think and behave freely for a specified amount of time.

3. *Defer judgment*: Lay aside judging whether an idea is worthy until later.

4. *Tag on*: When you've run out of ideas, go back to your list and make more out of the ideas you already have. (All adapted from *The Universal Traveler* by Don Koberg and Jim Bagnall [Los Altos, CA: William Kaufmann Inc., 1981], p. 82.)

This shouldn't be an everlasting process. Allow yourself ten to fifteen minutes for a brainstorming session and see where it leads. You'll be surprised at the amount and kinds of ideas you generate in such a short time.

With your list in front of you, consider the following questions. They may help you decide on which ideas to pursue.

- *What ideas make you smile?* Some ideas hit us just right. When shopping for furniture with my husband, we make purchases based upon whether the choice makes us both smile. It is rare, but when it happens, we know we're onto something!
- *What ideas make you cringe?* We naturally have aversions to certain ideas. A wagon wheel coffee table comes to mind for me! Or anything that reminds me of living in a college dorm and not a grown-up house.
- *What ideas make you ambivalent?* Some ideas don't hit me at all. If someone says, "What do you think of that?" and all I can think is "Whatever," that's an ambivalent idea. Be careful— some people mistake ambivalence for approval. So avoid saying, "I don't care what you decide" unless you really mean it.

Now that you've come up with some idea of how you want to arrange your current space, it's time to get to work and put your design solutions into action.

DIVE IN!

Up until this point all of your space planning has been mental. Now is the time for action. Although you will be tempted, don't organize anything yet. The idea is to first get everything in the vicinity where it belongs. Begin again with the room by room approach. Put everything in the room where it should be. Get it near its final resting place, and you can sort it all later.

Everything in Its Space

Choose a room with which to start. As you stand in the living room or dining room, pick things up and take them to the room they really belong in. For example, are there children's toys or school books that actually belong in your daughter's bedroom or your newly designated school area? Put them there. Is there laundry stuff in the kitchen or kitchen stuff in the laundry room? Put things where they belong. Put books near a bookcase.

Every Space Is Negotiable

Many of our spaces can have more than one function. Multipurpose rooms are not only popular but are efficient uses of space. Consider as well using a traditional space for something nontraditional. For example, if you already tend to pile school stuff in the dining room, why not consider transforming your dining room into a legitimate school area? Are you willing to say, "We don't need a dining room—we don't use it anyway"? Why not put your children together and use the other bedroom as a school area? Why not use screens to define a work space in the living room?

Eliminate Wasted Steps

The time we have with our children is precious and fleeting. If we can organize our space in such a way that we cut down on wasted steps, we should. Our laundry room is down in the basement, which greatly increases my steps. There's really nothing I can do short of expensive remodeling, but there are other space choices I can make in my home that will eliminate wasted steps. The boys' computer was originally in the basement in my office space. Their constant up and down during school was distracting and wasteful. We moved the computer to the main level in their bedroom, and now it is not such a hassle to do science and state history (the subjects they do on the computer).

SPACE—THE FINAL FRONTIER

Organizing the space in which we live and work can be liberating. Instead of feeling like you are stuck with a particular floor plan or square footage, you can take control so that the space serves the needs of your family. Our personalities, preferences, learning needs, and willingness all contribute to how successful we are at redefining our surroundings.

CHECK IT OFF!

Heart Matters

❑ 1. I must learn to be content with the space I've been given.

❑ 2. I believe that if God has called us to homeschool, He has already provided us with what we need—including the space.

Mind Matters

❑ 3. I desire our homeschool space to be more public/private.

❑ 4. The space serves our needs, not the other way around.

Body Matters

❑ 5. I will organize our space in a way that best suits our needs.

❑ 6. I will change the function of a traditional space if necessary (a dining room doesn't have to be a dining room).

Organize Your Supplies
and Materials

Now that you can see everything you own, it's time to deal with the mess. It's time to make decisions about all those piles, because everything you see is not going back into that space! For many people, sorting through what they own can be very difficult. Indecision takes over, and the easiest solution seems to be to just put it all away again without sorting. There are some emotional reasons we have trouble giving things up, and there are some spiritual reasons why we must. At this point you've already come so far, and now I encourage you to go all the way!

We are all attached to the things we own. Some things remind us of a different time and place. There are some things we keep though we don't remember why—we've just always had them. Then there are those things we think we might use someday, so we hold onto them just in case. How much you choose to keep depends on your storage capacity as well as your current and future needs. As you begin this process of sorting, keep God's perspective in mind. God doesn't want you to store up earthly treasures. God wants to know if you're willing to give up personal possessions. God wants you to know that you can be content with a lot less, and

He wants you to know that He will provide for your needs. How do those piles look to you now?

Sort It Out

Following the room by room approach, we can deal with each space in an organized fashion. At this point the idea is to move quickly, and not to ponder over each item too long. The system for sorting uses the One-third Rule. One-third of what you see will be given away or sold at a garage sale, one-third will be taken to the dump, and one-third will be put back into its designated space.

• *Pile One:* Decide if a particular item is reusable. Can you give it to another homeschooling family to use? Can you sell it at the used curriculum sale or garage sale? Sometimes we still have things either our children outgrew or we bought but never got around to using. Many families need curriculum, art supplies, chemistry sets and the like but cannot afford them. Maybe what you have will meet a need for another family.

• *Pile Two:* This next pile is for things that are either unusable or are just plain trash. It is quite liberating to throw things away. There's no need to feel guilty if you first sought to give away unwanted items.

• *Pile Three:* What remains is what will return to its designated space.

This sorting process can take two days or two weeks depending upon how much uninterrupted time you have. I highly recommend including your children in the process, especially when it comes to their own spaces.

A Place for My Stuff

The adage "Form follows function" especially applies to organizational systems. Many of us get into trouble when we buy a shelving system only to find that it doesn't suit our needs or is not the right size. Wait to choose a system until after you have sorted your belongings, and you'll know better what you need and its size. Just because something looks good doesn't mean it will function the way you need it to. And sometimes what functions best won't please the decorator in you. My family owns a great deal of books, not unlike most homeschooling families. Yet we didn't have the money to buy the amount of bookcases we required. Instead we built bookcases out of eight-foot boards and decorative concrete block. We stained the boards and even painted some of the blocks. That definitely met our organizational needs in many areas of the house, even though to me it looked like college dorm living!

Whatever you choose to organize, your materials should be based on these factors:

- Will it perform the needed storage function?
- Can we grow with the system, or will we outgrow it too soon?
- Can we afford it?
- Is it aesthetically pleasing?

Sometimes there's not already a system that we can buy to suit our particular needs. Sometimes we must create a system of our own. Actually, creating your own system is probably the more efficient use of your time. So often we buy storage systems that we end up selling at our next garage sale or bypass altogether. For example, the shoe organizer I bought. It sits there on the floor of my closet, and yet my shoes never make it back there. They are strewn all over the closet floor just as they were before I bought it! So now my husband will build one for me, although I'm afraid that he may just use board and decorative concrete block again!

Everything we've discussed thus far can be applied to any and every area of your home. However, homeschooling materials take up an incredible amount of space and are used just as often as the dishes in our cupboards. What are some of the materials we store?

Books, Books, and More Books!

Whether fiction, textbooks, or reference, we homeschoolers probably spend more time and money on books than non-homeschoolers. Because we value them, we must be diligent to keep them in good condition, maintain an accurate inventory of what we have, and keep them accessible. Many times we begin a unit of study and pull together all the resources we need from the library, friends, and bookstores, only to find we already had some of the books. Why didn't we notice them in the first place? Most likely because they were buried under socks! The storage of books is probably one of the most common complaints of homeschoolers. I keep waiting to open a door into a well-stocked library like in Disney's *Beauty and the Beast*®, yet I still sit here with many books still in boxes.

Art Supplies

The younger the children, the more art supplies you own. Even if you don't feel particularly adept in the creative arts, you will want to provide your child with some art experience. This then leads to clay, fingerpaint, tempera paints, chalk, brushes, string, etc. Art supplies do not stack as nicely as books do. It is difficult to store supplies that don't have common shapes or sizes. Some families, discouraged by the mess and difficult storage, abandon art altogether. They look for a class for their child instead. There's nothing wrong with that choice if it meets your child's need. But keep in mind, lack of storage doesn't have to mean lack of experience for your children.

Office Supplies

We use a variety of office supplies in our homeschools. Printer paper, paper clips, pencils, pens, markers, crayons, colored pencils, staples for the stapler, tape, construction paper, and notebook paper are just some of what we use on a daily basis. Where can we keep it all? Shouldn't we have an adequate supply of these things so we don't run out in the middle of a project? Where do we store the extra supplies?

There are many other supplies and materials that you as a homeschooler may use over the course of a week. If you now have everything near its designated space, you can inventory all your supplies at a glance. Commit to storing them in such a way that you will always know what you have.

Julie Morgenstern, author of *Organizing from the Inside Out* (New York: Henry Holt & Co., 1998), gives us one tip that is almost magical: Put things nearest their place of origin. Always keep in mind the function you have designated to a particular space. If school happens at the dining room table, all of your materials and supplies should be as close to that space as possible. Running up and down stairs to retrieve tape, a science reference book, and paper may improve your calf muscles, but it wastes time and energy.

BUCKETS AND BOXES AND BINS, OH MY!

Everyone has suggestions for how to store your stuff. California Closet Company® makes a lot of money saying that their way is best. Rubbermaid® and Tupperware® both make their millions storing our stuff. Organization is big business, but you don't have to break the bank to live a more orderly life. Denise Schofield, author of *Confessions of an Organized Homemaker* (Cincinnati: Betterway Books, 1994), suggests four different storage options. It's not a matter of what system you use, but that you think about your options:

• *Hang it up:* Here you have a multitude of possibilities. Pegboards, hooks, rods, nails, and even wire baskets can provide out-of-the-way storage. There are even baskets made by Rubbermaid® that hang on the wall—great for storing children's daily work.

• *Store it on the floor:* Although floor space is a precious commodity, there are probably overlooked and underused floor spaces in your home. Consider the spaces in between appliances or furniture. Look under things and behind things. Not sure what to do with your dear daughter's artwork? Store it in a flat shipping box behind a desk, between two bookcases, or under the bed.

• *Drop it in a drawer:* Although dropping things in drawers sometimes is like dropping things into a black hole, the option is still viable. The trick is to use drawer dividers. Anything that is hollow and rectangular (or square) is a potential divider. School supplies such as pencils, pens, markers, paper clips, etc. are all good candidates for drawer storage as long as dividers are employed. Stand-alone drawers, whether cardboard, plastic, or wicker, are also efficient storage units.

• *Shelve it:* This is probably the most popular storage option; yet some homeschooling paraphernalia don't seem conducive to shelf storage. The answer is to combine drawers or bins with shelving. Plastic rectangular baskets in a variety of sizes and colors are ideal for this storage option. This way you can store not only books but art supplies, manipulatives, and the like in baskets or bins on those shelves.

What you have and how much of it you have will determine the specific storage unit. Consider all the options. Look up at the walls, down on the floors, in between, under, and behind things in your quest for storage possibilities. Efficient use of space is not limited to the 900-square-foot home. Large homes are notorious for poor storage choices. The more space you have, the more stuff you will need to store.

STORAGE AND REAL LIVING

As you keep your eyes open for storage options and their containers, there are some lifestyle considerations that will make your choices easier and more effective. Homeschooling families don't necessarily conduct school between 9 and 3 but often continue into the evening and over the weekend. If one of our goals is to help our children become self-directed, independent workers, we must set them up for success by making their work accessible and manageable.

Portable versus Stationary Storage

If you can devote one room to homeschooling, then most, if not all, of your supplies will be permanently stored in that space. However, many of us cannot devote one room to homeschooling and must turn our dining room or kitchen table into our school area on a daily basis. Portable storage helps make this possible. Caddies used for cleaning supplies can be used for school supplies. Plastic baskets with handles can be used to tote each child's work from room to room if necessary. Even if you have one designated space for school, there may be times when school becomes portable. For example, what if you travel and want the kids to continue school, or if someone else cares for your children on a particular day and they must bring their schooling with them? A backpack is ideal as portable storage.

Within View and Within Reach

I must admit that I honestly prefer storage that is concealed. I like doors on cabinets and dislike open shelving for the most part. Yet, if everything was put away at all times, our children wouldn't feel free to get what they need when they need it.

KEEPING EVERYTHING IN ITS PLACE

Maintenance is usually much easier and less time-consuming than dealing with a mess that is out of control. If you now have storage units and therefore a place for everything, keeping it all there takes just two simple rules. First, do it daily. When you're done with school for the day, go ahead and put everything back where it belongs. Do it before you do anything else. Second, teach your children to be responsible for returning items or materials they used to their homes. Consistency is the key!

There are a few challenges to maintaining this sensitive balance. Those of us who have control issues may view the following as mere annoyances, but others will be completely overwhelmed.

Incoming!

Have your children started some sort of class outside your home? Did you change curriculum recently? Even moving from the elementary years to the secondary school years can increase the amount of "things" you must organize. Any change to your existing schedule will also put a burden on the system. Are you prepared? Don't be tempted to just start a pile for this new activity or curriculum; put it into your system immediately. I realize that one pile in a normally well-organized home doesn't seem like a big deal. But as we all know, piles have a life of their own and they grow! And they tend to congregate in groups!

Forgetful Family Members

You've trained them. You've nagged them. You've even bribed them! Yet somehow our spouses and children don't seem to place the same importance on our newfound organizational skills as we do. It is so tempting to do it yourself. Somehow that's less painful than a confrontation. But in the long run it adds more stress to your life and robs them of an opportunity to learn responsibility! Continue modeling organized behavior, and continue gentle prodding. Don't give up, and don't give in!

Illness, In-laws, and Itineraries

The bottom line is that life gets in the way of our best intentions. How organized does your house stay when you're sick? Admittedly, it would stay more organized if our children were in school full-time. But the reality is, our children are home most if not all of the day. If you are in bed with the flu, just be grateful that they got some of their schoolwork done without you and forget the rest.

Visitors, whether expected or not, will cramp your style. Sometimes we don't feel as comfortable in our regular routine with visitors around. Try to stick to your organizational habits, but leave that battle for another day if it will ruin a relationship. If Grandma wants to spend time with the kids instead of doing school, let her. That relationship is important.

Periodic vacations or other travel may be good for the soul, but they make it quite difficult to get back into a routine upon return. Allow yourself some time to ease back into your schedule. Sometimes we need a vacation from the vacation before we dive back into real life.

At this point in the process of organizing your homeschool, you are involved in the day-to-day details. These details threaten to overwhelm us and can discourage us from the ultimate goal of living a more organized life. It's a journey, and right now you are in the middle of the most challenging part of that journey. Sorting out all that we own is both intimidating and liberating. When you're done, what remains is freedom.

CHECK IT OFF!

Heart Matters

❑ 1. God expects me to be a good steward of all that He has given us—including materials and supplies.

❑ 2. I am willing to be content with a lot less stuff!

Mind Matters

❑ 3. Efficient use of space is important, no matter what the size of our home.

❑ 4. A cluttered home makes for a cluttered mind!

Body Matters

❑ 5. Creating our own storage system is cheaper than buying one.

❑ 6. In order to maintain the system, everyone in the family must know how.

7

Organize Your Paperwork

During my *Organized Homeschooler* workshops I ask everyone to write down their greatest organizational need with regard to homeschooling. After the workshop I separate these slips of paper by category. Inevitably the largest pile is about paperwork. "What do I do with all the paper we generate?" We must maintain our children's schoolwork in such a way that it is accessible and understandable. There may be a time when we will be asked to produce evidence of their work. Portfolios are ideal for this task.

As luck would have it, I am married to a professional organizer who at one time sold filing systems. My husband, Chip, has organized everything from art supplies to math papers. His filing principles appear below. You will notice that he does not recommend a particular system for you to purchase. As with space planning, discussed in previous chapters, form must follow function. Your system will be unique to your particular needs. Keep the following principles in mind.

FILE, DON'T PILE

Look around your home. Do you see any piles? How often do piles get smaller? The nature of piles is that they *grow*! At times this seems unavoidable. Piles seem to serve a purpose. We think that having like items in one place is being organized. All it really means is that we are too tired, too distracted, and for some of us, too lazy to put things away. Life is incredibly busy, but the saying "Pay now or pay later" really applies. You're either going to deal with the mess now or later. Deal with it now and it's manageable. Deal with it later and you will hate every minute of the task. So commit today to getting rid of the piles you already have and preventing future piles.

Break Things Down into Manageable Categories

That box full of school papers is an opportunity to categorize. When our son was small, he used to dump out four or five 100-piece puzzles onto the floor into one big pile. I learned quickly that this wasn't an act of defiance but a game to him. He would then spend the next hour or so sorting the pieces by the puzzle to which they belonged. Children love to sort! We've all had the shape sorter toy in our home. Kids love to figure out where things really belong. They love order! So instead of sighs and groans when faced with the paper pile, smile and treat it like the game you played all those years ago.

There are certain natural categories that homeschool paperwork falls into. You may have some that are unique to your own situation, but there are basically two main groups: papers our children generate and papers we generate. Within both of these groups are subcategories.

Papers Our Children Generate

Reading, writing, language arts, science, social studies, and math are all subject categories. You can even get more specific with comprehension, handwriting, spelling, health, and state history. It depends entirely on what you are studying. Take time to make a list of all the categories your children's work falls into. Hold onto this list—you will need it later on.

Papers We Generate

Lesson plans, support group newsletters, state guidelines, lists of all sorts, and even notes and reminders can be easily categorized and kept in a three-ring binder with dividers. If you sign your children up for lessons or a community sports program, there's paperwork that goes along with it. If you enroll a child part-time at a traditional school, there will be school communications to file. If you are expected to keep records of attendance and lesson plans for your state, there must be a place for those things as well. Even if an umbrella school maintains grades for your child, you will have your own copies to hold onto. Test scores and other forms of evaluation must also be documented and filed. Again make a list of all the categories your paperwork falls into for later use.

FILE FOLDERS ARE CHEAP

Walk down an office supply aisle in any discount superstore and you're sure to find a multitude of colorful, specially decorated or uniquely made file systems. Although color is important when it comes to organization, plain manila file folders are both cheap and effective. They do the job that needs to be done. So before you invest in the new neon-colored, plastic-coated file folders that come in their own handy container, ask yourself if you are willing to continue buying these folders for as long as you need to file. The system will only work if you keep buying the same parts and pieces. Can you afford that? If you can and are willing to keep up appearances, then buy it. But if money is an issue and you intend to homeschool for a very long time, consider plain manila file folders instead.

FANCY, COMPLICATED SYSTEMS
USUALLY DON'T WORK

Every year I buy new inserts for my Day-Timer® calendar. It took years for me to find one that suited my daily needs. Now that I have one that I like, I will always use it. The same can be said for file systems. We are attracted to sleek, complicated systems that promise to meet all our filing needs. We buy them but find out quickly that they do no such thing. Beautiful color-coordinated file cabinets are still just that—file cabinets. And file cabinets only *hide* files—they don't organize them. As with space planning, it is better to sort all your papers, categorize what's left, and then purchase a system that contains what you keep in the most efficient manner.

DO IT DAILY/WEEKLY

The easiest way to avoid piles is to file daily, or at the very least weekly. Having an in-basket of some kind takes care of daily needs, but make it a weekly habit to put your children's papers into whatever system you've created. We keep best-work portfolios, and every Friday our boys sort their work from the week into this portfolio. That way there is never a mountain of schoolwork to go through.

HAVE FILES VISIBLE AND
ACCESSIBLE

File cabinets are the traditional storage unit for paper. However, once that drawer is closed, you have no idea what is really in there. If you can't see your files, you won't think to use them. If the cabinet is tucked away somewhere, again you won't use it. Consider also your children's role in maintaining the files. In order to encourage them to participate, they should understand the system and have no trouble accessing it.

COLOR

The more paper you keep, the more reason you have to use colors to file. Assigning a color to each category will make it much easier to retrieve paperwork and to file new paperwork. In addition, the more children you have, the more effective color can be. Five children? Use five different colors for their files or their lesson plans or schedules. If you use three-ring binders, assign a different color to each child. We have two boys. Christopher's materials are blue, and Charles's are usually red. Their binders, spiral notebooks, and folders are color-coordinated. If any of their stuff is sitting on the table, I know who it belongs to! Color just makes the job easier.

SIMPLE ENOUGH FOR KIDS TO UNDERSTAND

Keep in mind that homeschool files are not akin to the files found in your doctor's office. For those of us who love the details, be careful you don't get carried away with the system and forget those the system is meant to serve. A good rule of thumb is that if the system is too difficult for your seven-year-old to use, it's just too difficult. A good system is a simple system.

PURGE OFTEN

In the beginning you will find that you keep everything. Every scrap of paper gets filed. How wonderful! However, try to look through your now well-ordered file system and see if there are papers that you can trash instead. In fact, purge even before you file. Keep only what you intend to keep permanently.

Follow these guidelines, and you are well on your way to organizing all those papers. This is a great life skill to teach children. That way when they're grown, they won't misplace their insurance policies, their child's immunization records, or their yearly tax information.

PORTFOLIOS

Whether you are required by law to keep one or desire to see for yourself what your child accomplished during the school year, portfolios are effective assessment tools. Not only are they one of the easiest file systems for student work, they are a means to instill pride in one's achievements. When children take pride in their work, they do a better job overall. Portfolios fulfill all the filing requirements we've discussed so far. They are easy to use, provide a simple system, and are accessible and visible, as well as inexpensive.

CREATING

Even when I was a teacher in a public school, I utilized portfolios for my students. I experimented with a variety of ways to store and showcase student work. After a number of failed attempts that just didn't make the grade, I realized that the easiest system for myself and my students was simply a basic three-ring binder. Use one for each child, and provide dividers for each subject that will be filed in this binder. The majority of children's work can be three-hole-punched. Invest in one of those as well.

Keep in mind the power of color coding, and give each child a binder of a different color. For a few pennies more you can get the kind with a top-loading plastic sleeve right on the front for a cover. Let your children design the cover of their portfolio for a personal touch.

MAINTAINING

Remember that maintenance is something best done on a daily or weekly basis. Every Friday our boys go through their work folders and choose their best work to put in the portfolios. If your curriculum uses quizzes or tests, put these in the portfolio. Spelling tests, handwriting samples, and reports are all good candidates for a portfolio. But what about that flip-book of how the digestive system works or the relief map of Italy they made out of wood and plaster of paris? If it can be folded, fold it and slide it into plastic sleeves that are already three-hole punched. If it can't be folded, take a photo of it and either mount it as you would in a scrapbook or scan it into your computer and add explanatory text.

FUN TOUCHES

If you have a computer, you can embellish your children's portfolios. Save to disk images of field trips, special projects, or performances. There are plastic storage sleeves just for diskettes. Turn your portfolio into an electronic portfolio. If you have access to the Internet, you can also create your own web site to showcase your children's work. If you don't have a computer, you can brighten up portfolios with artwork or stickers. Give your children a chance to use rubber stamps, die-cuts, and even glitter glue to make their portfolio a personal reflection.

SHARING

Your children worked hard all year and showcased their best work in this personalized three-ring binder. Take it a step further and share their work with others. In some families dads are barely aware of what their kids are doing while at home. Set time aside as a family so that each child can sit down with Dad and show him what he or she learned. He will be amazed, and the children will have a healthy pride in their work.

If you want to make an even bigger deal of the end of the school year, invite family and friends over for a student-led conference night. Serve food. Make it special. Then give full attention to all the children as they share their portfolios and what they learned. Allow time for those invited to ask the children questions. Prepare your children that questions will be asked. Watch them blossom right before your eyes!

Even if you choose not to utilize portfolios, find some orderly way to keep and showcase your children's work. Some families even create their own books of their children's work that become permanent keepsakes. Who knows, they may even come in handy someday when your child applies for a special program or even college!

Storing homeschooling paperwork is not just an activity to complicate your life. If you value your time and your children's time, make all their work count. Don't give them something to do that isn't worth keeping. Trashed work equals wasted time and wasted effort. What are you willing to do to show your children that you care about their work? Isn't it worth a few extra minutes to file it for safekeeping?

CHECK IT OFF!

Heart Matters

❑ 1. If the governing authorities require me to maintain a portfolio, I willingly submit to that God-given authority.

❑ 2. Keeping my children's work in an orderly manner shows them that I care about what they do.

Mind Matters

❑ 3. Categorizing paperwork is the first real step to getting it organized.

❑ 4. The simpler the system, the better it will work.

Body Matters

❑ 5. I will maintain the filing on a daily or weekly basis.

❑ 6. I will train my children to maintain their own portfolios.

8

Organize Your Family

The degree to which your family is organized is dependent almost solely on you! I know that doesn't seem fair, but it's true. If you can't get your act together, you won't be able to expect the other members of your family to get their acts together. Personalities aside, orderly families are trained, not born. Organization must become an integral part of daily living, not something you put on just while doing school. We can encourage it by our own examples, by intentional activities, and by creating an environment within our homes that sees orderliness as a blessing and not a curse.

There are practical reasons for you to train your children in orderliness. First and foremost, you are training them as future husbands and wives. What kind of husband or wife do you want your child to grow up to become? It's obvious to me that my mother-in-law did an excellent job training her son. I bless her whenever I can! Another reason to cultivate orderliness in your family is the mere fact that you can't do it all alone, and you shouldn't be expected to do it alone. I remember vividly a friend telling me how worn-out she was from maintaining her household by doing every job alone. I was appalled! She had three daughters over the age of ten who did nothing. Even if you have the gift of orderliness, you do your children a disservice if you don't share that gift with them.

There are many reasons people give for not training their children to be orderly.

• *If I want something done right, I'll do it myself.* We've all felt this way at one time or another, but some of us feel this *all* the time. Keep in mind two things: (1) You're probably right—they might not do it as you would. But (2) they'll never learn if you don't give them the opportunity. Sometimes it is more important for your child to learn how to do something than it is for it to be done right.

• *It takes so long to teach someone else to do what I do that it's not worth it.* As a teacher and parent, I'm painfully aware of how long it takes to teach someone a skill I might take for granted. It takes patience, and it takes time. If you are rushed, that may not be the moment to teach your son how to clean the bathroom. However, if you find that you are always rushed for time, it may be your priorities that need to be addressed. Keep in mind that some children (and spouses) take longer than others to learn a particular skill. Are you willing to give them the time they need?

• *My children are too young to really help.* Many parents mistakenly think that children must be at least ten years old before they can contribute to maintaining a home. We don't give kids credit for what they can do. An eighteen-month-old can pick his clothes off the floor and put them in the hamper. A three-year-old can carefully carry his plate to the kitchen. A four-year-old can empty wastebaskets. There are age-appropriate chores. Teach them early, and they will consider doing chores to be a normal part of family life. And as my mother lovingly says, "Isn't that why we had kids?"

• *I was brought up to think that it was my job, not my family's, to maintain a home.* I am half Italian, and whenever we would go to my grandmother's for dinner, it was expected that the girls and women would clear the table, do the dishes, and serve the coffee and dessert while the boys and men hung out in the living room waiting to be served. My family was insulted when my husband (who is 100 percent Italian) rose to clear the table on one visit. What was worse was the fact that I didn't get up to do the dishes. Whether it is cultural or simply the way you were raised, I would encourage you to consider the following statement: "This is *our* home, and *we* take care of it." We've all been called to stewardship of our homes and everything in them.

ORGANIZED FAMILY OR ROBOTS?

Years ago there was a movie about perfect wives and perfect children living in a perfect neighborhood. It was called *The Stepford Wives*. The horrific twist to this movie was that they weren't real people—they were robots. Sometimes we can desire order so much that we turn our families into robots. We expect extraordinary behavior and attitudes, and when we don't get it, we are incredibly disappointed. There is sometimes a thin line between running an orderly home and crushing the spirit of those who live in it. The danger of legalism is very real.

How can we avoid turning to this obsessive extreme? The most important thing we must do is to humble ourselves before God. We need to realize that we are not perfect ourselves and that nothing we do on our own can please Him. There are also practical lessons to learn:

• As homeschoolers we have more time to train our children to work around the house. Don't let that opportunity slip by.

• Good, hard work improves a bad attitude. If your child is having trouble staying on task with his schoolwork, give him physical work to do and let him work out the attitude.

• The more children you have, the less work you could be

doing. I no longer clean bathrooms, mop floors, dust, or fold laundry. I have boys who do that!

• Straighten a child's room and it will be clean for a day; teach a child how to straighten and now it's his job!

• When you say that everything has a place, make sure everyone knows where that place is.

• Do not pay children for daily maintenance jobs around the house. These are expected as good stewardship. Pay instead for unusual or less common jobs.

• Don't expect your children to be organized if you haven't taught them how.

In her book *Simplify Your Life with Kids* (Kansas City: Andrews McMeel Publishing, 2000), Elaine St. James gives us the real reason we should all strive to live a more ordered and simpler life: "Raising happy, healthy, well-adjusted children is one of our greatest challenges. Kids require incredible amounts of our love, understanding, patience, praise, nurturing, guidance, respect and thought. And these things all take time. If you can simplify even one or two areas of your life, it will vastly improve the quality and increase the quantity of time you have to spend with your kids. And your family life will be much easier and a lot more fun. As it should be."

Emilie Barnes, author of the *15 Minute Home and Family Organizer* (New York: Inspirational Press, 1998), reasons: "We are to live life with a godly purpose. For many years I thought I was raising children for the moment, not realizing that I was teaching for generations to come. The things I taught my children are now being taught by them to my grandchildren. Time flees from us so quickly. We pause for a moment, take several deep breaths, and find ourselves to be grandparents and great-grandparents." Time is short. Teach your family how to redeem it, and you will affect generations to come!

THE SPILL-OVER EFFECT

One aspect of education is *generalization*, which means that when you teach a child a particular skill, he or she will transfer the use of that skill to many other areas of the curricula or to his or her life. This is not unique to the traditional educational setting. If we diligently teach our children the skills of organization, they will inevitably use those skills first in the environment in which we taught them and then beyond. Organization becomes a habit of mind before it becomes a habit of the body. But you can be sure that what you teach them about how to run an orderly home will spill over into becoming organized students and later, organized homemakers.

How can we ensure that these organizational skills will transfer to their schoolwork and to their life beyond us? It has to become an expected part of their daily life first. That takes time and repetition. It has to become second nature. Don't just teach them once how to keep their room straight and then expect it all the time. You'll only frustrate both of you. For something to become second nature, it must be taught over and over again. Our tendency is to fall back on our bad habits; so we must diligently reinforce the good ones. For example, did you ever try a new diet and then slowly fall back into your bad eating habits? It takes time to change, and oftentimes we don't give our families the time they need to develop new organizational habits.

A TRAINING APPROACH

As a former teacher I tend to borrow strategies from the educational world, but I only borrow the ones I know work. One such strategy is used when teaching a new concept. It was one of the first things I learned in my teacher training, and it is so basic that I never forgot it. When introducing a new skill or concept, if you want the student to permanently integrate the skill into his thinking, you do it in steps. Below are the steps put into the context of training for orderliness with your family:

• *Step One: Show & Tell.* First explain how to use the organizational skill. Then show your family how it's done.

• *Step Two: Do It Together.* Explain again how it works, and then do the skill with your child. This should be done a number of times before moving on to the next step.

• *Step Three: Supervised Practice.* Give directions once again, but this time watch your child do it himself. If he makes a mistake, correct him and allow him to finish the job. This step takes the longest amount of time. It is very important that you witness your child doing the organizational skill correctly and consistently.

• *Step Four: Independent Practice.* This is the hardest step! Give directions for the task, and then walk away while your child does the job. Initially you should tell your child to come get you when he's done so you can inspect his work. He shouldn't come get you unless he is sure he did his best job. Offer both correction and praise. Later you can expect to assign the task, give a time frame within which it should be completed, and walk away knowing it will be done.

Admittedly, this is a time-consuming process. Yet in the long run you will save time by first teaching your child how to do it right. I remember when we taught our two boys how to clean their rooms. It was a skill we had to teach and reteach over a couple of years. However, now I know that when I tell them to straighten their rooms, they will do it the way that is expected. Sometimes I inspect their work; sometimes I don't. This skill has spilled over into how they maintain their school baskets. Every day they sort their work into appropriate folders, and every Friday they choose work they are especially proud of to put into their portfolios. That

way on Monday we start with a neat, organized basket just waiting
to be filled with the week's work. I'm grateful that I don't have to
do this for them. I'm especially glad that I took the time to train
them in the details. I also have the satisfaction of knowing that
when they are employed someday, they will attend to the details of
that job as well. Why? Because it is second nature now.

ROUTINE AND TRADITIONS

We all have a certain way of doing things on a regular basis.
Routines are behaviors done out of habit. Traditions are also done
out of habit but with attached meaning, sentimental or otherwise.
Sometimes when we examine why we do what we do, it changes
us for the better. Mindless routine or rote tradition are rarely considered positive. But tradition steeped in emotional attachment and
meaningful routine improve the quality of life. Our children
depend heavily upon routine and tradition. A home minus these
all-important aspects encourages children to look elsewhere for stability. As we look into organizing our families, we must also consider the benefits associated with concepts such as limits,
discipline, routine, and tradition. Each of these ideas communi-
cates stability and belonging to family members.

How can we communicate that stability without coming off as
drill sergeants and hopefully rarely using the phrase, "Because I
said so!"? Guess what? It takes *time.*

• When introducing a new routine, limit, discipline, or tradition, *take time to sit down as a family to discuss what will change
and why.* It may already be meaningful to you, but it must be
meaningful to your entire family before any lasting change can
occur. I remember a number of "we've got to tighten our belts"
family meetings when I was growing up. We all had to expect
less and curb our spending in order to survive when my father
was out of work. Each such discussion did two things. It made

us all feel like we were a part of what was going on, and it eliminated disappointment that things weren't going our way or we weren't getting the things we wanted. We all understood. It had meaning.

• *Keep up an open dialogue*, so family members can voice their concern or frustration with the new routine. That way they are less apt to sabotage the effort, and you can adjust the expectations where needed. A child has to feel safe enough to say, "I'm frustrated!" Sometimes we expect too much. Our oldest son has experienced this frustration on more than one occasion. When I make a change on how we maintain something in our home and I don't communicate it clearly, he will inevitably do it the wrong way. Then, of course, I get angry and disappointed. Just because I have it all figured out doesn't mean my son does, and it shows. He avoids the task or makes excuses about why he can't do it just then. That's my cue to stop and ask him what's really going on. More often than not, he just didn't understand how he needed to do the job or it was too difficult for him.

• *Make routine changes slowly and in small doses.* You may have the big picture and can see sweeping changes you want to make right now in your home. However, trying to change everything at once invites disaster! Pick your battles carefully. Choose the thing that will impact your family's quality of life the greatest, and work to change it. Then go on to the next. The idea is to keep everyone's frustration levels at a minimum.

Over a period of time you can implement new routines, start new family traditions, and set new limits. This is a process, not an end result. It takes time, commitment, and prayer. As you begin making changes in how you homeschool, you will see these changes reflected in how you manage your family and home and vice versa.

GET OUT WHAT YOU PUT IN

If you are interested in a comical yet true-to-life account of how to manage your family in an organized fashion, read the book (or listen to the audio tapes or watch the film) *Cheaper By the Dozen* by Frank B. Gilbreth, Jr. and Ernestine Gilbreth Carey (Bantam Doubleday Dell Audio, 1994). As the title indicates, these parents organized twelve children! Those of us with three children or less bow down before those with a large family. For those with children closer to a dozen, you will be encouraged and inspired by this wonderful classic. It helps to see other families in action. Some of us work very hard to make what we do look easy. There are good role models out there in churches, in support groups, and in your neighborhood.

The amount of change in your family is directly related to how much effort you put into enabling those changes. If you do nothing, nothing will change. Children don't magically figure out how to keep orderly rooms or offer selflessly to do chores and do them well. They must be carefully taught. The key word here is *carefully*. I could also have used the word *attentively*, *cautiously*, *gingerly*, or *guardedly*. All of these words indicate a level of reflection and deliberateness.

Just as our own creation was intentional and not by chance, an organized family is created, not born. It is a choice, something that is planned and nurtured. We must be attentive to our family's needs, cautious not to overorganize, gingerly pointing out faults, guarding our tongues and being wary of anyone or anything that says they have all the answers.

CHECK IT OFF!

Heart Matters

❑   1.   I must be careful that my desire for an organized family doesn't become a legalistic set of rules.

❏   2.   I'm not raising children for the moment, but for genera-
           tions to come.

Mind Matters

❏   3.   My own attitude can help or hinder this process.

❏   4.   I understand this is a time-consuming process.

Body Matters

❏   5.   It's a matter of show and tell. They're watching my show
           every day!

❏   6.   Establishing routine and tradition is worthwhile.

9

The Task of Reorganizing

Guess what? Once you've gotten everything in your life as organized as you desire, it is bound to fall into chaos over time. Does that mean that the system you chose wasn't good enough? Does it mean that you aren't the home manager you thought you were? Does it mean that psychologically you wanted it to fail? Nothing so deep as any of these suggestions. The truth of the matter is a spiritual truth (and a scientific one): Due to the sin of Adam, nothing can be maintained without toil. Everything on this earth is in a state of decay. Scientists call this phenomenon *entropy*. Left to its own, any system will eventually fail. That's why we have system managers. And guess who is the system manager in your home? You are! The woman of Proverbs 31 is described as the keeper of the home. Her husband is praised because of how she manages her household and family.

Given the circumstances, the creator of the system also maintains the system. Eventually you will train your children to maintain the organization, but in the beginning you are the main manager. I am blessed with a husband who is very organized and oversees the organization of our home. However, his example is what has encouraged me to be a more organized homeschooler. But many families do not have husbands with the gift of organization. If you have been given that gift, minister it one to another (1 Peter 4:10).

How do you know when it is time to reorganize? What does it take to get back on track? What kinds of changes should you make? The good news is that reorganization takes very little effort in comparison to your initial task of organization. So be encouraged!

SIGNALS AND SIGNPOSTS

There are a multitude of reasons why your orderly lifestyle is falling into chaos. Major life changes inevitably mess with routine. As a person who thrives on organization, I met the birth of our second child head-on as an organizational challenge. Even before he was born I sat down to contemplate the impact this new addition would make on our household. I knew his schedule would be different. I knew my laundry would increase. I knew where we went and when we went would be altered. I knew I would not get much sleep. I made a tentative schedule that coordinated with our eighteen-month-old's schedule. On paper it looked manageable. But as you know, life doesn't happen on paper.

Charles arrived and for some reason did not naturally fall into the well-ordered routine I set for him. If it were up to him, he would have slept all day! I also didn't count on his brother's reversion to the time of his infancy. He didn't sleep! The household chores were forgotten, meals did not magically prepare themselves, and sleep was a faraway dream. Chaos in all its glory! After six weeks of shock, things eventually returned to normal, schedules and all. But meal preparation was still a challenge. So I had to find a new way to manage that task, and the answer was not to order pizza on a regular basis.

Whether it is a new baby, a move, a marriage, a new job, or even a loss of some kind, adjustments must be made. Families with their own businesses or a spouse who works at home are especially susceptible to falling into chaos. As a homeschooler, your children's own needs may dictate a change in routine or schedule. If you are used to homeschooling one child and your youngest is now of school age, then you are adding to your schedule. What if you homeschool three children and one is starting traditional school? You may have to transport that child. You may choose to volunteer in his school. Your time will have to be re-prioritized. It is a process of continual adjustment.

The key is to recognize the changes that are needed and face them head-on. Don't avoid them hoping that everything will just work out. That rarely happens.

TAKE A MENTAL INVENTORY

What types of adjustments need to be made? Consider the following:

• *How long does it take to do school each day?* Are you finding that it is taking longer and longer to accomplish school daily? Are there so many interruptions that school takes a backseat? Are you tending to the *urgent* over the *important* more often?

• *How much schoolwork gets accomplished each day?* Even though you follow a lesson plan, are you putting off things until the next day, which turns into the next week or even the next month? Do you notice that most of what your children do for school they do without you, and you're not quite sure how much of it they really learned? Is your oldest spending more of her time teaching the youngest and not learning her own studies?

• *Does your spouse comment on the state of the house?* Does your husband gingerly ask why the house is always a mess? Maybe he even jokes about it. Would you happily invite an unexpected visitor into your home, or would you make an excuse not to open the door any farther than you have to? Do you have overdue library books because you've misplaced them?

• *Do you feel anxious or doubtful about homeschooling?* Are you overwhelmed to such a point that you think maybe putting one of your children in a traditional school will give you the breathing space you need? Do you feel inadequate because you're not accomplishing what you hoped you'd accomplish? Are you looking for other opportunities for your children in the form of classes or a co-op so that someone else can teach the bulk of the subjects?

• *How is your and your family's health lately?* Is your son/daughter complaining about physical pain more and more often? Is it becoming more difficult to get your children or even yourself up in the morning? Have your children's eating habits changed? Is anyone having trouble sleeping? Are you cooking less and less and buying takeout more and more?

There may be other symptoms personal to your own situation. Become sensitive to changes in your children's attitudes and behaviors. If motivation decreases or tempers flare, there is a good chance that something is wrong. These are all symptoms of increased stress. How well we manage our homeschools determines the stress level in our homes.

PICK YOUR BATTLES

What if you've waited too long? What if things are out of control? You desire to restore order as quickly as possible. But that is not the smartest route to take. Things didn't fall apart all at once. They won't be fixed all at once either. Choose the issue that has the greatest impact upon your quality of life and homeschool experience. When we moved across country, our school schedule was affected on a large scale. We lost weeks prior to moving, and it took weeks after moving for us to get back on track. At times I felt guilty that we weren't getting school done. In fact, I became so anxious that I considered putting our boys into a traditional school so that (1) I could get things done, and (2) they could quickly make friends and therefore adjust to their new surroundings. Even though I was incredibly stressed, I chose not to take such a drastic measure and tackled the task of reorganizing our home and homeschool one day at a time.

What issue is the most pressing? What level of order do you need in order to function? What will alleviate the greatest amount of stress? Everyone has a different tolerance level. For me, things looking unfinished causes me a great deal of stress. So when we moved in, we unpacked all the necessities immediately. What we couldn't get to went into the basement, so I wouldn't have to look at it. Then I could turn my attention to school. What is important to you may not be important to your neighbor or even your spouse. But if you are the one responsible for managing the home and your children's education, then it is the most important issue.

SET PRIORITIES

There are just so many hours in a given day. We must be discerning about how we spend that time. If things have come undone, there's a good chance that priorities have been either forgotten or ignored. We're all busy, and this is not only a characteristic of a woman of the twenty-first century. The Old Testament reveals a woman in Proverbs 31 who was quite busy as well. We would do well to examine her situation. Below you will find the passage from Proverbs. Each verse is also paraphrased, and a modern-day comment is offered as well:

> [10]*A wife of noble character who can find? She is worth far more than rubies.*

> *Character is worth more than money. She exhibits strong character.*

(Character is the main issue.)

[11]Her husband has full confidence in her and lacks nothing of value.

Her husband has faith in her character and therefore has everything.

(Her husband has it all because of his wife's character.)

[12]She brings him good, not harm, all the days of her life.

She does not harm him in word or deed.

(She doesn't nag him, malign him, or throw dishes at him from across the room.)

[13]She selects wool and flax and works with eager hands.

She is eager to make some of her own things with her own hands.

(She takes classes to learn how to make things from scratch.)

[14]She is like the merchant ships, bringing her food from afar.

She goes to a great deal of trouble to bring the food to her home.

(She goes to the farmer's market for the best vegetables instead of the grocery store.)

[15]She gets up while it is still dark; she provides food for her family and portions for her servant girls.

She gets up before everyone else and prepares them breakfast.

(She is up at the crack of dawn preparing food for everyone, even her own maid or cook!)

¹⁶She considers a field and buys it; out of her earnings she plants a vineyard.

She is an entrepreneur or has an at-home business.

(She is good at Internet trading or has her own Mary Kay® business.)

¹⁷She sets about her work vigorously; her arms are strong for her tasks.

She does her work with great energy and is strong.

(She stays fit and pumps iron so she can physically do all that she needs to do.)

¹⁸She sees that her trading is profitable, and her lamp does not go out at night.

Her business is profitable, and she is always prepared in case things change.

(Her Internet trading is going well, but she makes sure she has a nest egg.)

¹⁹In her hand she holds the distaff and grasps the spindle with her fingers.

She makes things from scratch.

(She makes her own clothes, knits her own things, even tends her own garden.)

[20]*She opens her arms to the poor and extends her hands to the needy.*

She is generous to the needy and reaches out when she can.

(She volunteers at a hospice or visits AIDS patients and sponsors a child in a Third-World country.)

[21]*When it snows, she has no fear for her household; for all of them are clothed in scarlet.*

She is prepared for winter.

(She buys quality clothes off-season and is always prepared.)

[22]*She makes coverings for her bed; she is clothed in fine linen and purple.*

She decorates her home herself and wears the finest clothes.

(She loves Home and Garden Television and does her own home decorating, which saves her money.)

[23]*Her husband is respected at the city gate, where he takes his seat among the elders of the land.*

Her husband is well respected in his place of business.

(Her husband on his own accord is respected, but the reputation of his wife increases his respect.)

²⁴*She makes linen garments and sells them, and supplies the merchants with sashes.*

She makes wares to sell.

(She makes things to sell at the Christmas bazaar.)

²⁵*She is clothed with strength and dignity; she can laugh at the days to come.*

She has strength of character, and she is not worried about the days to come.

(She has strong faith that waves off worry.)

²⁶*She speaks with wisdom, and faithful instruction is on her tongue.*

When she speaks, it is with wisdom. She gives faithful instruction.

(She can be counted on to speak with wisdom, and she teaches those in her charge well.)

²⁷*She watches over the affairs of her household and does not eat the bread of idleness.*

She manages all household affairs and is not idle.

(She is aware of all that goes on under her roof and is sensitive to the needs of those who live there. She doesn't sit and watch the afternoon talk shows.)

²⁸*Her children arise and call her blessed; her husband also, and he praises her.*

Her children bless her with their words, as does her husband.

(Her children think they have the "best mom in the world" and tell her so.)

[29]*"Many women do noble things, but you surpass them all."*

Her family considers her the best!

(Like Ralph in *The Honeymooners*, they say, "Honey, you're the greatest!")

[30]*Charm is deceptive, and beauty is fleeting; but a woman who fears the LORD is to be praised.*

A charming personality is deceptive and beauty goes, but a woman after God's own heart is to be praised.

(She is the real thing. Her faith is her strength and is worthy of praise.)

[31]*Give her the reward she has earned, and let her works bring her praise at the city gate.*

She deserves praise for the things she does.

(God will say in the final day, "Well done, good and faithful servant!")

—PROVERBS 31:10-31

I realize that the woman of Proverbs 31 is intimidating to say the least, but so is Jesus. We know that we cannot reach such perfection here on earth. The call is to become aware of what God praises and to aspire to do those same good things. Elisa Morgan, president of MOPS International, commented on this passage in the *Mom's Devotional Bible* (Grand Rapids, MI: Zondervan, 1996): "Whether or not the Proverbs 31 woman is one spectacular woman or a composite of several women, we can take heart from the truth that few of us can ever exhibit all of these qualities at once. And God does not expect us to. What he desires is that our attitudes and actions are yielded to him whether we're sitting at the city's gates or by the home fires."

Look to this list of qualities and see which ones you can work on today. If things are falling apart, there's a good chance that many of these qualities are not in place. Are you yielded to God?

RELAX! BUT ONLY FOR A MOMENT

Do you ever feel like you're running on empty? At the end of any given day you notice that you still didn't have time to sit with John to do his history report, Jessica is still on the same math lesson as she was last week, and the laundry is still on your bed (with another load in the dryer and yet another in the washer). All you can feel is tired, and oftentimes you feel defeated. The closest thing to a vacation for you is sitting in front of the television or the computer until the wee hours of the morning. Trying to keep things organized is both tiring and trying. And when we do it in our own strength, we will run out of steam! God has some tips for the home organizer. Considering the source, they are worth the time.

- *"Be still, and know that I am God"* (Psalm 46:10). We are so busy orchestrating the day that we forget to spend time with God. We give Him our leftover time, which is usually quite minimal. If we take time to sit and be still in His presence, we will be better able to know His will. If you have yet to schedule in that quiet time, consider giving Him the firstfruits of your day instead of what energy you might have left at the end of it.

- *"I will give you rest."* Know that He has it all under control. Rest in that truth. "Come unto me, all ye that labour and are heavy laden, and I will give you rest. Take my yoke upon you, and learn of me; for I am meek and lowly in heart: and ye shall find rest unto your souls. For my yoke is easy, and my burden is light" (Matthew 11:28-30, KJV). God asks that we come to Him for rest—not to the television or the Internet or even a good book. This isn't to say that these things are off-limits, but don't use them as an escape. God is our refuge and strength. When we choose to "veg out," we leave room for the enemy to corrupt our thinking. So as you look to be rejuvenated, focus on the things above by going to God's Word. Pray in the quiet spaces, and He will give you rest.

- *"Love the Lord your God with all your heart and with all your soul."* "Thou shalt not hearken unto the words of that prophet, or that dreamer of dreams: for the LORD your God proveth you, to know whether ye *love the LORD* your God with all your heart and with all your soul. Ye shall walk after the LORD your God, and fear him, and keep his commandments, and obey his voice, and ye shall serve him, and cleave unto him" (Deuteronomy 13:3-4, KJV, italics mine).

Sometimes it seems so hard to know what to do about any given situation. Yet it is easier than we think. When questions arise about how we should set our priorities or how we should use our time, the guidelines are within God's Word.

THE GREAT MANAGER

Earlier I said that the one who establishes the system is also the manager of that system. We are only part of God's system, the one who is the Great Manager. Our human bodies are made up of multiple systems, and our spiritual body acts in the same way. We have all been given great gifts that work within God's system. Since God ordered the universe and it is His plan of which we are a part, let's go to Him continuously for guidance.

The task of reorganizing will arise again and again. It is a matter of maintaining the system you already have in place.

• Be sensitive to stress levels and changes in your lifestyle.

• Decide what needs to be adjusted based upon how much that will impact your family.

• Make sure your priorities are lined up with God's.

• Spend time with God to gain guidance and confidence.

• Make your changes.

In time this process will become more or less automatic. You will become increasingly sensitive to the needs of your family. You will watch your children's learning increase and your ability as a teacher improve.

CHECK IT OFF!

Heart Matters

❑   1.   I know that everything created is in a state of decay, even my own organizational habits.

❑   2.   When things fall apart, it is just a delay or a detour, not destruction.

Mind Matters

❑   3.   The stress level in our home rises dramatically when the system falls apart.

❑   4.   I can only address one organizational need at a time.

Body Matters

❑   5.   When things go wrong, it's time for me to recheck my priorities.

❑   6.   I must spend more time with God!

10

Habit Forming

Why do you wait until the end of the school year to sort your children's papers?" I asked a good friend on the floor surrounded by mounds of papers from her four children. Jayne looked agitated, her eyes darting from pile to pile.

"I really hate this time of year," she said. "It's overwhelming how much stuff I have to sift through."

"Then why do you do it this way?" I asked.

Without hesitation Jayne said, "I've always done it this way. In our five years of homeschooling, I've always done it this way."

So often we do what we do out of habit. The question begs to be asked: "Why?" Up until this point we've learned that what we do is first determined by what we believe and what we think. So the answer "Because I've always done it that way" is unacceptable. It's make it or break it time!

THE POWER OF HABIT?

According to the *Macmillan Dictionary for Students*, "a habit is an action that has become nearly automatic through deliberate or unconscious repetition." Habits are powerful; they define our character. If someone considers me a punctual person, it is probably because I am consistently on time. Conversely, if someone considers me a liar, it would mean that I habitually lie. Even when we label our children, we are pointing out their habits. When we diagnose a child as hyperactive, it means that he or she habitually has difficulty sitting still or attending to any given task. And when we label a person as disorganized, it means that he or she does things in a disorderly fashion on a regular basis. Our habits reveal our character.

The good news is that even though habits are powerful, they are not all-powerful. They can be broken and made anew. As human beings, our habits, and therefore our character, can be changed. The idea is to change for the better.

HABITS OF HEART

What are some habits God discourages? By His character we know he is omnipotent (all-powerful) and immutable (never-changing). His habits define His character. Some other things we know about God include:

- God is good.
- God forgives.
- God is merciful.
- God is patient.
- God is faithful.
- God is orderly.

Since He has given us the best example to follow, we are called to form godly habits, to be like Him. And as we lead our children, they will follow the character we have shown to them. Homeschooling provides more time to develop character than if children were in a traditional school setting. But character isn't taught out of a textbook; it is taught by both deliberate and unconscious example. It's taught out of habit.

God encourages habits that are like His own character. And since God is love, much of His character is revealed in 1

Corinthians 13:4-8. If I were to replace "love" with my own name, I would see the character and habits God encourages me to have:

Vicki is patient,
Vicki is kind;
Vicki does not envy,
Vicki does not boast,
Vicki is not proud.
Vicki is not rude,
Vicki is not self-seeking,
Vicki is not easily angered,
Vicki keeps no record of wrongs.
Vicki does not delight in evil but rejoices with the truth.
Vicki always protects,
Vicki always trusts,
Vicki always hopes,
Vicki always perseveres.
Vicki never fails.

As you can see from this list of character traits, God encourages all these habits. The last one, "never fails," does not refer to never making a mistake but rather means failing to allow the Law of God to have authority in our life (see *Vine's Expository Dictionary*). Without this last habit, the others cannot be cultivated.

God also *discourages* certain habits in our lives. Our sinful nature indulges in many deliberate and unconscious practices. Fighting against it is a continual struggle. Paul often wrote about this. He exhorts us to:

• "Fight the good fight" (1 Timothy 6:12).
• Focus on things above (Colossians 3:2).
• Work heartily as unto the Lord (Colossians 3:23).

These and many more commands show us that we must deliberately make new habits. These new practices will help us over-come evil (bad habits) with good (good habits). Keep this verse in mind as well:

> Not only so, but we also rejoice in our sufferings, because we know that suffering produces perseverance; perseverance, character; and character, hope.
>
> —ROMANS 5:3-4

Persevere means "to continue steadfastly in a course of action or pursuit in spite of difficulties or obstacles" (*Macmillan Dictionary for Students*). We must make a habit of perseverance.

HABITS OF MIND

> And be not conformed to this world: but be ye transformed by the renewing of your mind, that ye may prove what is that good, and acceptable, and perfect, will of God.
>
> —ROMANS 12:2, KJV

What do you think about on a regular basis? Even within the context of homeschooling, what we think about determines what we do. Whether the thoughts are deliberate or unconscious (as our definition for *habit* proposes), they control our actions. Here are some common thoughts from homeschoolers:

Thought: I think homeschooling is the only way to ensure a moral upbringing.
Possible Action: I teach character development more than academics.

Thought: I think homeschoolers excel above and beyond their traditionally schooled counterparts.

Possible Action: I give my child a standardized test annually to prove this to family and friends.

Thought: I think that no matter how little I do with my children, it is still more than they would get in a traditional school.
Possible Action: My children learn what they need to learn when they need to learn it. We have no real plan.

Thought: I think there is no reason good enough to put your child back into a public school setting.
Possible Action: Even if I need help, I would never go to a public school to get it.

Thought: I think my children will learn all they have to learn eventually.
Possible Action: I don't dictate what my children should learn. I let life teach them.

Some positive actions can come from the above-mentioned thinking, but often it is the negative actions that we notice. If you are willing to cultivate new habits of thinking, you will organize your homeschool differently. Paul has one other exhortation about how we think:

> *For by the grace given me I say to every one of you: Do not think of yourself more highly than you ought, but rather think of yourself with sober judgment, in accordance with the measure of faith God has given you.*
>
> —ROMANS 12:3

Do you think there is only one way to homeschool and it's your way? If so, there's a good chance that you think of yourself more highly than you ought.

HABITS OF BODY

Remember how my friend Jayne always waits until the end of the year to go through her children's school papers? That's because she *believes* it's all right to procrastinate and then *thinks* that it doesn't matter anyway. What if she believed in redeeming the time and thought that *does* matter? Most likely her actions would show it. She wouldn't wait so long. The previous chapters discussed what we do to manage time, space, supplies and materials, paperwork, and our families on the whole. Habits of body are all the things we do on a regular, routine basis with regard to homeschooling. Here are some of the things I do:

- I make lists for my boys every Sunday night.
- I read the lesson before they do.
- I take them to piano lessons weekly.
- I take them to enrichment classes weekly.
- I go through their papers with them weekly.
- I pray with them daily.
- I keep our materials in the same spot daily.
- We have a "how are we doing?" breakfast conference approximately every six weeks.

I know I do some things unconsciously at this point, but much of what we do is deliberate. We are practicing the habit. *Practice* may be used of either a person or a group and applies to an action that has been made a habit deliberately and by choice (*Macmillan Dictionary for Students*). We practice what we think and believe. We all, in effect, practice what we preach. What do your practices say about what you think and believe?

HABITS AND HOMESCHOOLING

Many homeschoolers equate habit and routine with a stifling, sterile environment in which to learn. They avoid it at all cost. But I encourage you to consider striking a balance between strict schedules and spontaneous pursuits. If an airline makes a habit of on-time arrivals and departures, we praise them. If they are chronically late, we are harshly critical and withdraw our business. Our job is to raise children in the way that they should go. If we don't model and encourage healthy and praiseworthy habits in the time we have them, how else will they learn?

It is a luxury to have our children home with us. There is time to give them all they need to walk in this world worthy of praise. Homeschooling provides some unique opportunities to experience and develop strong positive habits. Consider the following activities:

A family business. Running a family business is quite common among homeschoolers. For those who have never considered such a venture and such a dramatic change in lifestyle, it is worth investigating. If the very thought causes trepidation, consider for a moment a business of a much smaller scale. The idea is to involve your children wholeheartedly in the start-up and running of the business. One family we know has a charter fishing boat business. Dad runs the boat, and Mom books the trips and takes care of the accounting end of things. Up to a certain point their children were familiar with the business, but they were mere spectators. Their mother thought it was time to learn for themselves how to run a business, including marketing, finance, and quality service. The seventh and fourth grader now create a newsletter and distribute it to their father's clients. They also take digital photos of each catch and make a T-shirt for the client to remember the trip.

What started out as a way to be involved in their dad's business has mushroomed into a new offshoot business that caters to all the boats at the marina. The children have learned to be consistent in the quality of their service and products. They have formed good habits that include skills such as reading, writing, graphic design, publishing, photography, and accounting, to name just a few. They have added to the family business in a way hardly anyone expected, though their mom is sure it was a direct answer to prayer!

A family church ministry. Maybe a family business is not within your realm of possibilities. But perhaps you or your spouse are involved in a ministry at your church that can include your children. Does your church feed the homeless? Do they sponsor a widow's workday of some kind? I've known families that serve in these ministries together. If there isn't a church ministry you can plug into, maybe you could start one. Maybe visiting a nursing home on a regular basis. Maybe collecting clothes or food to bring to a shelter. Maybe sponsoring a child overseas. All of these ministries require commitment and a willing heart. They require good habits.

A family volunteer effort. Habitat for Humanity, Save Our Shores, and Adopt a Highway are just a few of the available volunteer efforts in communities across the nation. There may be local efforts with which you can volunteer as a family. Look around in your community, and pray that God will reveal to you where He wants you and your family to serve. But remember, once you are involved, people count on you; so again, commitment is required.

A family mission trip. Many homeschoolers are full-time missionaries. In fact, that may be the very reason they homeschool. However, you don't have to sign up for full-time missionary work to serve in this way. Many churches sponsor short-term mission trips. Depending upon the ages of your children, the sponsoring organization may be open to entire families going on such a trip. I know a homeschool family who went on a short-term mission trip to El Salvador with their two daughters, ages eleven and nine. Both girls got to see their parents in action and learned for themselves the commitment it takes to go to the mission field.

There are other ways you can teach your children how important habits and commitment are in service situations. These are just a few suggestions to get you started.

BAD HABITS TO BREAK

We are all pestered by bad habits during our homeschool day. Become aware of them, and then deliberately set out to break them. These might include:

- I do not plan on a regular basis.
- I regularly run errands in the middle of the school day.
- I use the same curriculum with all my children because it is easier for me.
- I don't monitor what my kids are doing since that's when I do my housework.
- I have never attended a support group meeting or a homeschool convention.
- I don't usually make the time to look over or grade my children's work.
- I don't have a set place to keep "school stuff."
- If something more interesting comes up, we'll skip school, even if it has nothing to do with what we're studying.

These are all issues of habit or routine. They just happen to be poor habits. You can probably think of more. Forming habits—the good and the poor—is what you do. Look at your habits without getting defensive, and consider the consequences that poor habits lead to for your homeschool. Be willing to make a change or two. After all, we are called to put off the old nature and put on the new. Remember that this is a process, not a weekend project.

GOOD HABITS TO MAKE

Conversely, we all pursue some good habits in our homeschools. These might include:

- I read aloud to our children on a regular basis.
- We start school at the same time each day if possible.
- I am available when the children need me. I put off chores until before or after school.
- I am always willing to try a new approach if what we're doing isn't working.
- Our children have daily chores.
- We normally stay home until our schoolwork is complete.
- We choose additional activities based upon their relevance.

Your list may look very different from mine. What we value is revealed by our list. On a regular basis, out of habit, how do you manage your homeschool? The answer should spur you on to bigger and better things.

Is it important that we oversee and even run our children's education in an orderly fashion? If our ultimate goal is to please God, then we desire orderliness. This is a choice. It requires perseverance. It brings hope. Without it we have no focus for our perseverance. Without it joy becomes something we chase instead of something that is bestowed.

CHECK IT OFF!

Heart Matters

❏ 1. My habits reveal my character.

❏ 2. God encourages habits that are like His own character.

Mind Matters

❏ 3. I must be willing to cultivate new habits of thinking before I can change the physical habits.

❏ 4. I believe there is more than one way to do most things.

Body Matters

❏ 5. I will commit to keeping our materials in the same spot daily.

❏ 6. I will commit to making lists or lesson plans for my children weekly.

❏ 7. I will reflect upon how we're doing at least three times a school year.

❏ 8. I will model for my children the habits I hope they will embrace.

11

The Nuts and Bolts of an Organized Homeschool

Although there are hundreds of ways you can organize your space, materials, and resources, the homeschool environment presents unique challenges. You can comb through a dozen books for just the right technique, but it's probably simpler to find out what other homeschoolers have done instead. Before we look at some homeschool organizational suggestions, consider these tried and true statements:

HANDLE PAPER ONLY ONCE

Although I admit breaking this rule almost daily, I believe in its wisdom. What I tend to do is open mail or collect my children's papers and put them somewhere else so I can deal with them later. The better idea is to deal with them right away and not procrastinate. Put things where they belong, whether in a file, a portfolio, or the trash. Take the few minutes right at that moment to take care of it before it piles up and becomes a project that takes an hour.

IF YOU CAN'T KEEP IT NEAT, YOU HAVE TOO MUCH STUFF

Every time I get frustrated with my children because they seem incapable of keeping their rooms in order, I realize this truth: The more stuff you have, the more difficult it is to keep it neat. Although the most obvious choice seems to be to create more storage area, it is the least popular option that makes the most sense: Get rid of a lot of your stuff! As homeschoolers we tend to hold onto things that have long outlived their usefulness, just in case. If you just can't bear to part with the kindergarten math manipulatives that your seventh grader once used, just in case you unexpectedly have another child, then at least pack it all away out of sight. Then if for some reason you do have that miracle child, you can pull it out when he or she is five. When you do decide to store your materials, curricula, and books for another time, clearly mark the boxes by subject. That way if you do need to retrieve something, you will know where to look.

IF YOU CAN'T SEE WHAT YOU HAVE, YOU WON'T KNOW WHAT YOU HAVE

So often our storage consists of either materials crammed into cardboard boxes and shoved into a closet or bookcases piled high with

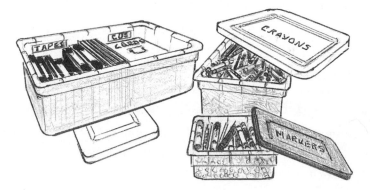

books one on top of the other. Bookcases are great, but make sure you line books up side by side with their spines facing out so you can see what they are. Group these books by subject so you don't waste a trip to the bookstore or library when you already have just what you need. Boxes are also wonderful, but how about baskets or clear plastic bins and boxes instead of traditional cardboard? They come in a variety of sizes and shapes to meet your storage needs.

IF YOUR SEVEN-YEAR-OLD CAN'T MANAGE YOUR SYSTEM, IT IS TOO COMPLEX

Some of us are so organizationally minded that we make our system of organization more complicated than it has to be. We love structure for the sake of structure. If your children are having difficulty maintaining the system you already have in place, more than likely it is too complex for them to follow. A child's logic doesn't usually measure up to an adult's. How can you eliminate steps in your system so it is more manageable for your youngest child? How can you communicate your system in kid language? Remember the acronym K.I.S.S.? For our purposes here, we can say Keep It Simple, Silly (that other word is unacceptable). God's system is simple, and His burden is light. Is yours?

ONLY KEEP OUT WHAT YOU ARE ACTUALLY USING

Those of us who are collectors have a difficult time following this suggestion. We like our stuff, and we like having it out to look at. When it comes to our homeschooling materials, supplies, and resources, we can lessen our organizational challenges by only keeping within reach and in eye's view those things we will use that year. You therefore have permission to store last year's stuff or next year's stuff in boxes in your garage, basement, or attic!

With these ideas in mind, you can tackle most of your organizational challenges as a homeschooler. The following scene is an example of one organized homeschool. Let's look at each component one at a time.

The following illustration gives you an overview of our own organizational structure. We utilize everyday storage items in our homeschool. Some of the characteristics of this space have been previously discussed.

- It is a dual-purpose space. It is both our breakfast room and our homeschool area.
- Bookshelves are used to store a variety of materials.
- All materials are easily accessible to the kids.
- Only the materials we are currently using are visible.
- The system is easy enough for the children to maintain.

Now let's look at each component separately.

Shelving is probably the most versatile storage solution for homeschoolers. Admittedly, shelves can easily become a catchall for everything, no matter its size or shape. Shelving can be purchased at a discount store or do-it-yourself store or can be constructed using a variety of materials. For years we could not afford bookcases, so we made our own. The easiest way to create shelving is to combine concrete block and wood boards. Although an obvious throwback to my husband's college dorm days, this type of shelving system is cost-effective, customizable, and easy to assemble.

Currently our bookcases store textbooks and bins with resource materials and assorted supplies. Because they are open bookcases, I strive to keep them orderly and attractive. I can see everything we have, and it is easy for our children to find what they need and to return it to where it belongs. Storage cabinets are a closed system of shelving. They are an inviting choice for homeschoolers because their closed doors hide a multitude of organizational "sins." Closing the door is not the answer to disorganization, although it was my own mother's answer to my disorderly teenage room!

Baskets come in all shapes and sizes and are made from a variety of materials. Plastic baskets, no matter the shape or size, are affordable and easy to find at any local superstore. Whether round or rectangular, solid or open weaving, baskets can serve almost every storage need. Before you purchase anything, sort through all of your materials and supplies. Throw away what no longer works, has missing pieces, or is no longer used. Then look at the sizes of what remains. Choose your baskets according to what materials will be stored in them.

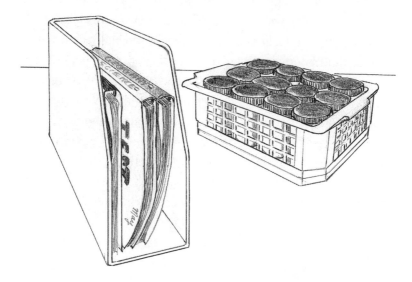

We use *plastic bins*, not unlike magazine storage boxes, for a variety of things. They help us store workbooks, guidebooks, and magazines spine out, standing up. Not only does this make it easier to see what you have—it is better for the books. We label the bins by subject and use them to sort materials for a specific purpose. When we were planning a trip to our nation's capital, we accumulated a lot of material on Washington, D.C., the White House, and the American Presidents and First Ladies. We put that material in bins. Prior to the trip, we studied what was in the bins. After the trip we used what we learned in a report about

Washington, D.C. Those bins kept us organized just by their very existence, and still do.

These stand-up bins can be cardboard, solid, or open-weave plastic and can be found at both office supply stores and area superstores like Walmart®. They are inexpensive and versatile. Again it is best to sort what you already have before buying any storage unit. A *flat surface* on which to work is a must-have for many homeschooling families. You might be wondering why I even include it in my organizational plan. I have met many homeschoolers who do school on the floor, on the couch, in their beds, outside, at the beach, in the car, or in an easy chair. Designating a tabletop for certain projects or tasks is not confining or disturbingly traditional or too "school-like." Choose the right place to perform the right function. I'm not advocating that everyone run out and buy an old-fashioned school desk for each child in their family (although many homeschoolers have them). I just want each homeschooler to feel free to choose whatever system works for them. And *I* need a table!

We have gone from being a one-table household to having a multi-surface home. We have a table in the dining room, a table in the sunroom, a table in the kitchen, a table in my office, portable tables in the family room, and yes, the old wooden drafting table in the basement. We are definitely not wanting for tabletops. When you purchase that new dining room table, keep the old one. Store it in the garage if you must, but keep it. You never know when you'll need an arts and crafts or model-building surface.

Our particular school area uses an old dining room table. It is a dual-purpose space. We use it for school (for one child because they can't all work within the same space), and we use it for breakfast because it is in the sunroom and it is just too beautiful in the morning not to eat there. When we have guests, it becomes the kids' table. But we didn't start out with so many tables. We started out with one dining room table (now the school/breakfast table) in a two-bedroom, 900-square-foot apartment. That table wasn't dual purpose—it was multipurpose! Yes, I had to clear their school stuff before each meal. No, I didn't leave my scrap supplies lying on it all day. It served many purposes, and as a reward we kept it when we bought a new one years later.

How do you store and showcase your children's work? We use *three-ring binders*. I've met people who use shoe boxes, document file boxes, accordion (expandable) file folders, and even a pizza box! The three-ring binder is affordable, easy to use, easy to view, and stores easily on a bookshelf. It's portable. It can be personalized. It's recognizable. We keep our portfolio binders in the back of our work baskets. That way when the week is done, we sort through the papers, three-hole-punch the ones we want to showcase, and put them in the binder. It takes five minutes!

Where you keep your children's portfolios will determine how often you use them. If they are out of sight, they are out of mind. If they are difficult to use, you won't use them. Keep your system simple, and keep it in sight.

The suggestions illustrated in this chapter work for our homeschool. They may or may not work for yours. As you visit with other homeschoolers in their homes, look to see how they organize their things. If you see something you like, take a closer look, ask questions, and try it out for yourself.

Admittedly, the more children you homeschool, the more difficult it is to manage all your materials. Only have out what you are currently using, and it will be manageable. If you're not using it, give it away or pack it away!

And remember, if you can't see it, you won't have it when you need it. How often has your eleven-year-old searched every room to find the dictionary that wasn't put away? How often are there pencils all over the house but not where your son sits down to do his work? Teach children to put things back where they belong so they will be there when they need them the next time.

CHECK IT OFF!

No matter the size of your home, you can learn from others how to keep things organized. Look around the area(s) in which you spend most of your time when you are homeschooling.

Heart Matters

❏ 1. I can do all things through Christ who gives me strength!

Mind Matters

❏ 2. I am willing to learn from others ways to keep things organized.

Body Matters

❏ 3. Is there a way to consolidate your materials into one space?

❑ 4. Do you have things out that you have never even used?

❑ 5. Is there a bookcase in your spare room that would be more functional in your school area?

❑ 6. Have you sorted through your materials before packing them in boxes?

❑ 7. Are your boxes clearly labeled?

❑ 8. Do your children know how and where to put things away when they are done with school?

❑ 9. Does everything have a place?

12

A Homeschool File System

Some families are file-friendly, and some are not. Personally, I don't know how people keep track of all the paper that comes into their homes without some sort of filing system. I guess it all ends up in the circular file (the trash can)! Yet as homeschoolers we are required to maintain at least some evidence of our children's school experience. How much you keep is definitely up to you, but if you don't have a system, things *will* be lost.

My husband worked for a file systems company at one point, and his organizational expertise was invaluable to his customers. Similarly, he has helped us create a file system to maintain our homeschool records in a way that is user-friendly, simple, and complete. Although not every system works for every family, you might want to adapt parts of our system to your homeschool.

THE WALL OF FILES

Once we graduated from our concrete block-and-wood, dorm-style shelving, we looked at ways we could maintain our ever-growing files. Every time we visited someone's home for the first time, my husband was curious about their filing system. What he found, much to his dismay, was that most people don't have one! When people visit our home, our filing system is his pride and joy. He takes visitors on a tour of our house and ends in our shared office to show off our wall of files. It is a combination of shelving and the plastic bins described in the last chapter. We use end tab file folders (as opposed to the more common top tab) so that they can be easily viewed without removing them from their shelf. Chip expects this system to be maintained so that when he shows it off, people will be impressed. And they are always impressed!

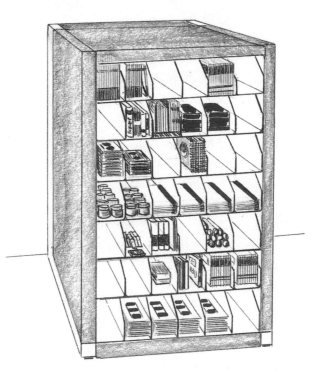

We store both our household files and our homeschool files in this system. As a writer, I have yet more files, and they too are stored on the wall of files. Teaching ideas, miscellaneous resources, and homeschool catalogs all have a home on the wall. Once there, you can label each bin by category, color code the file folders themselves, and even reorder the bins according to ease of use. I can take a bin down from the wall for a closer inspection of its contents. I can add a bin at any time as long as I have shelf space. This system is probably the most efficient way to store all of our paperwork. We often wonder what everyone else does with their stuff!

FILE BOXES

Document file boxes—the ones that you assemble, with a top and punched-out handles—are invaluable for long-term storage. Using boxes of the same size makes the job even easier. They are easier to stack, move, and transport if they are the same size. When we moved from Florida to Colorado, Chip didn't depend upon the kindness of strangers or the leftover boxes from the grocery store to pack and transport our belongings. He ordered a couple hundred boxes from a box company to do the job. I know that may sound excessive, but it was relatively inexpensive, and it made packing so much easier and loading the moving van a breeze.

We use the document file boxes for the majority of our educational materials and books that we are not currently using. They are labeled and stored in the basement. That way when I'm planning a unit on flight, I go to the science boxes and look for the flight box. Similarly, I have grade level material in boxes marked for a specific grade level. When the school year is done, I box up what we studied that year along with the boys' work files and portfolios and mark it with the appropriate year. If I need to go back and find something later, I'll know exactly where to look.

THE HOMESCHOOL ORGANIZER

One of the common characteristics we have for many of our storage solutions is whether or not it is portable. The school baskets can be carried from room to room, taken into the car, and brought to my husband's office if necessary. The bins on the shelves can be taken down, inspected, and returned without disturbing the order of the system. The children's portfolios can be carried easily anywhere they need to have them, whether it is to show grandparents, teacher evaluators, or other homeschoolers. Because portability is important to the homeschooler, we have devised a way to store and organize your child's day-to-day work in an attractive, orderly container.

The components of the Homeschool Organizer are simple yet effective. If you choose to create one yourself, it is important to first determine its purpose, its components, and its affordability. The main component is the expandable folder itself. There are many versions from which to choose in an office supply store. Choose according to your child's specific needs. If he or she is in early elementary school, you may not need one that expands as wide as the one we use.

The Homeschool Organizer

- Manila folders with fasteners to maintain daily work
- Expanding wallet files to house manila folders
- Identification info
- Front utility pocket to hold disks or accompanying supplies such as labels, Post-It® notes, and flags.

V. CARUANA, 2001

The next components are the file folders. Top tab folders work best. You may choose to color-coordinate your file folders, but it isn't necessary to the success of the system. It may be easier for you to keep track of what is whose if you use one color for one child and one for another. Our youngest uses red for as many things as he can. So his folders would be red in this case.

Determine whether or not you need additional storage capability. Do you need to store computer disks, artwork, or pencils and pens? What about a calculator or a ruler? Decide what your child needs on a daily basis and choose an expandable folder that has the ability to store those things. Some come with outside pockets of varying shapes and sizes. Choose what you will use.

The Homeschool Organizer makes your child's work portable and keeps it organized. The older he gets, the more he will have to keep organized. If you are traveling with your children and plan to do work on the road, consider this system. Transport their textbooks (if you use them) in a separate canvas bag or backpack. Do whatever it takes to make life simple, yet keep things in order.

FILE FOLDERS WITH FASTENERS

If you can't already tell, we love file folders. Maybe it's because Chip sold them for a living for a few years, and we were surrounded by them on a daily basis. Actually, we love them because they actually serve our organizational needs—and they're cheap! So far we've talked about file folders with regard to color and whether they are top or end tab. But there is so much more!

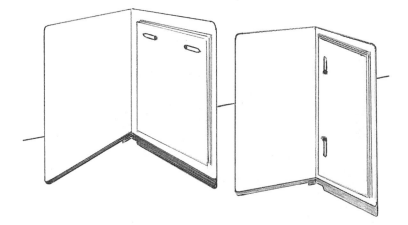

Let's talk about fasteners. As a homeschooler, much of what you will put in a file folder should be stored in chronological order.

So often we throw papers into a folder without a second thought. Yet they don't magically sort themselves. And if they do somehow get filed in order, they won't stay that way. They will also fall out upon removal from the shelf. Fasteners are the answer!

File folders can come with the fastener option. Keep in mind that if you choose these folders, you will need a two-hole punch as well. The fasteners can be placed in a variety of positions. Traditionally coded as positions #1 and #3, a file folder with two fasteners is ideal for homeschooling papers. You can even buy dividers that fit onto the fasteners if you need to categorize the papers you put into the folder. I haven't gone that far, but the fasteners themselves are invaluable. Now our stuff is in order because I hole-punch them and put them in right away. They also stay where I put them!

I've given you specific ways to file your homeschool paperwork. If you are not a file-friendly person, I strongly suggest you make friends with a file system. You don't have to use every suggestion; just choose something that will make your life easier and your paperwork accessible and keep you accountable.

CHECK IT OFF!

You may be tempted to use the circular file as your primary file system, but you will miss out if you do. Throwing things away is a good idea if it has a purpose. Throwing things away just to clear the countertop may be foolish. Take the time to go through those unwieldy paper piles, file all that you want to keep, and throw the rest away. Maintaining a system for your homeschooling papers has many advantages. Check off the ones that will especially benefit you and your family.

Heart Matters

❑   1.   A filing system creates order out of chaos.

❑   2.   It shows your children you value their work.

Mind Matters

❑ 3. It saves precious time when you need to find something in particular.

❑ 4. It encourages accountability.

Body Matters

Some of the suggestions for filing that were reinforced in this chapter were (check the ones most appealing to you):

❑ 5. File folders are an inexpensive way to store homeschool paperwork.

❑ 6. File folders with fasteners are even better!

❑ 7. Three-ring binders offer solutions to a variety of paper storage problems.

❑ 8. Document storage boxes are worth using for long-term storage.

❑ 9. Keeping files on a bookcase or some other wall system helps us to use the system every day.

13

The List of Lists
for
Homeschooling

If you are a list maker, then this chapter is for you. If not, consider the suggestions here and choose what will work best for your homeschool. Or make up your own lists! Making a list helps you organize your thoughts, keep track of your intent, and gain a feeling of accomplishment when you check things off. Following are examples of many different lists that can be utilized by homeschoolers. Some formats may be new to you; others may already be a part of your daily routine.

LIST OF GOALS

Whether you make academic goals, process goals, spiritual goals, or a combination of all three, write them down. The following list is an idea list for each type of goal. Use what you want, or use them as a starting point to create your own:

Academic Goals (what)	Process Goals (how)	Spiritual Goals (attitude)
Learn & recite multiplication tables	Write numbers legibly	Complete work without complaint
Learn & recite addition facts	Write cursive with appropriate slant, size and spacing	Honestly evaluate how well work was completed
Able to +, −, x, / fractions	Complete a 25-problem timed math facts test within 45 seconds	Be willing to help younger siblings without complaint
Learn cursive hand-writing	Be able to stay at work independently for more than 20 minutes	Be faithful to complete agreed upon tasks
Know basics of state history	Use a variety of sources when writing a report	Persevere even when the task is difficult
Able to use parts of speech correctly	Type a 400-word report	Use self-control to stay on task
Write a simple sentence	Write a topic paragraph with creativity	Be open to suggestions from others about your work habits
Write a simple sentence	Write a friendly letter neatly	Forgive siblings or Mom quickly
Write a compound/ complex sentence	Recite a poem by memory with emotion	Be patient until it is your turn to work with Mom
Write a complex sentence	Finish all work in a timely manner	Be kind to siblings when they do poorly
Able to group animals by mammals, reptiles, amphibians, birds, etc.	Stick to a predetermined deadline to complete a project	Be happy for siblings when they do well
Able to tell time	Use pencil for math and do it neatly	Answer Mom with respect at all times
Able to measure using inches, feet, yards	Use pen for language arts and do it neatly	Speak to siblings with kindness
Type 30 words per minute	Type 30 words per minute with 90% accuracy	Forgive yourself when you do poorly

LIST OF CURRICULUM CHOICES

Once you make a list of goals, you can match curriculum choices to those goals. Group your goals (academic) by subject, and then look at curriculum, resources, and materials that meet those goals. There is not one curriculum that meets all goals. As you consider what to purchase for the next school year, keep your list nearby. If you go to a homeschool convention, bring your list with you so you are focused while you shop. Here is a sample of a curriculum/goal list:

Goal	Subject	Grades	Curriculum/Resource/Material
Be able to learn & recite multiplication facts	Math	2-4	Saxon, Math-U-See, Singapore Math, Miquon Math
Be able to learn & recite addition facts	Math	2-4	Same
Be able to solve real life problems using math	Math	2-4	Same
Be able to integrate reading, writing, grammar, and handwriting	Reading/ Language Arts	4-6	Alpha Omega, Sonlight, Konos, Weaver
Be able to study the classics with a Christian world view	Reading/ Language Arts	4-6	Same
Be able to study grammar, etc. through the use of novels	Reading/ Language Arts	4-6	Same

Goal	Subject	Grades	Curriculum/Resource/ Material
Study American History through biographies	History	3-6	BJU, A Beka, Sonlight
Study Leaders of the Faith as part of history	History	3-6	Same
Study an accurate portrayal of American History	History	3-6	Same
Study Chemistry with hands-on experiments	Science	5-8	Sonlight, MicroChem Kits, Alpha Omega
Study Physics with hands-on experiments	Science	5-8	Same
Study Biology with hands-on experiments	Science	5-8	Same
Study Human Reproduction with a Christian world view	Science/Health	5-8	Same

SHOPPING LIST FOR BUYING SUPPLIES, ETC.

Homeschool supplies can be purchased in a variety of ways. Keep track of where you purchase these supplies and materials. You can use this list to help you shop, or use it to keep an account of what you have and where you purchased it.

Material	Company	Price	Source	Contact
Old Testament History	Green Leaf Press	16.99	God's World Book Club Catalog	800-951-BOOK

LIST OF STANDARDS OR LEARNING OBJECTIVES

Many homeschoolers strive to become aware of the learning objectives outlined for each grade level. Even homeschoolers who create their own curriculum desire to consult these standards in an attempt to stay focused. This is not for everyone. If it matters to you and you are not even sure what standards and learning objectives look like, consider the table below. Each state has created its own list, and you can choose standards and objectives from their lists or use them as a starting point from which to create your own. You can check the Department of Education's web site for your state to view its standards. Below are some general standards to get you started.

	Grade One	Grade Five	Grade Eight
Mathematics	Students will use concrete materials to demonstrate the meanings of halves, thirds and fourths of sets and wholes.	Students will locate commonly used positive rational numbers, including fractions, mixed numbers, terminating decimals through thousandths, and percentages, on the number line.	Students will determine the two consecutive whole numbers between which the square root of a whole number lies *(for example, the square root of 72 lies between 8 and 9)*.
Reading	Students will be able to retell information in a logical, sequential order including some detail and inference.	Students will be able to identify supporting details and main idea.	Students will be able to paraphrase, summarize, synthesize, and evaluate information from a variety of text and genres.
Language Arts	Students will dictate or write stories that have some evidence of beginning, middle, and end.	Students will write compositions that show some attention to the proper use of parts of speech.	Students will make limited, but appropriate use of technical terms and notations in writing.

	Grade One	Grade Five	Grade Eight
Science	Students will state simple hypotheses about cause and effect relationships in the environment.	Students will recognize that forces of gravity, magnetism, and electricity operate simple machines.	Students will identify and analyze ways in which advances in technology have affected each other and society.
Social Studies	Students will recognize own state as a part of the 50 states.	Students will recognize that the world is made up of many peoples who have similarities and differences to their own.	Students will explain the development of the U.S. as a nation to include the struggles, accomplishment, and roles of individuals and/or groups as the U.S. emerged to be a leader of nations.

RUBRICS AND CHECKLISTS

Rubric as an educational term describes a sort of checklist of skills or expectations. Rubrics are most often used to evaluate student work and to help students evaluate their own work. As a homeschool parent you can use rubrics for evaluation but also to help guide your child to becoming an independent worker. If you and your child agree on the expectations of a particular assignment, you can then help him to monitor his progress by giving him a rubric. You can create a rubric for almost anything. For example, the elaborate rubric below is for a basic report. It allows both the child and parent to evaluate the report.

	CHILD		PARENT	
	Yes	No	Yes	No
TITLE/COVER PAGE				
Is the title centered?				
Is the title properly capitalized?				
Is the name properly placed?				
Is the date properly placed?				
REPORT/BODY				
Does it have an introduction that gets the reader's attention?				
Does each paragraph have a main idea?				
Does each paragraph include supporting details?				
Is the report arranged in sequential order?				
Is the report easily understood?				
Is it written in your own words?				
MECHANICS (Fewer than _____ errors)				
Is correct capitalization used?				
Is proper punctuation used?				
Are complete sentences used?				
Are all words spelled correctly?				
Is correct grammar used?				
Is the report neatly written? Typed?				
Is the report of sufficient length to convey the information?				
ILLUSTRATIONS				
Is there a minimum of _____ illustrations included to explain the information?				
Do the illustrations have captions or labels?				
Are the illustrations neatly done?				

	CHILD		PARENT	
	Yes	No	Yes	No
BIBLIOGRAPHY				
Is there a minimum of five sources listed?				
Is there a minimum of three different types of sources?				
Is the correct bibliographic form used?				

Rubrics can be created in all shapes and sizes depending upon the purpose for which they are created. You could use Post-It® notes for rubrics that list only a few expectations, or you could use full-page rubrics as illustrated above. What you put on the rubric is up to you and your child.

There are other lists you might also want to consider keeping.

• List of Current Inventory of Supplies
• List of Homeschool Contacts
• List of Homeschool Conferences
• List of Homeschool Publications
• List of Area Support Groups
• List of Retailers That Offer Educator Discounts

Can you get obsessive about list-making? Of course. Keep in mind that a list of any sort is only good if you actually refer to it. If it just ends up as one more thing to file, it is a waste of paper. Create a list for the sake of organization, not for the sake of list making.

CHECK IT OFF!

List-making is a great organizational tool. The mistake most people make is to make a list that is too long. If your "to do" list is too long, you will be quickly discouraged as you notice all the things you did *not* accomplish that day. It's much easier to start small. You can always add to a list. Even when you list expectations on a rubric for your child's work, keep in mind that the more you expect, the more likely your child will be disappointed in his performance. You can always raise the bar, but begin by fostering success with a list that is manageable for both of you.

Heart Matters

❑ 1. I believe that list-making will encourage more orderly thinking.

Mind Matters

❑ 2. I think it is one organizational tool worth using.

Body Matters

This chapter presented the following lists. Choose the one(s) most important for you to implement today!

❑ 3. List of goals.

❑ 4. List of curriculum choices.

❑ 5. Shopping list for buying supplies.

❑ 6. List of standards and learning objectives.

❑ 7. List of skills or steps (rubrics).

❑ 8. List of current inventory of supplies.

❑ 9. List of homeschool contacts.

❑ 10. List of homeschool conferences.

❑ 11. List of homeschool publications.

❑ 12. List of area support groups.

❑ 13. List of retailers that offer educator discounts.

Final Thoughts

The quest for organization begins in the heart. Your desire to live a more orderly life will be honored because it is in accord with God's will for you. One of the keys to becoming a more organized homeschooler is found in that very word *becoming*. It is a gradual process. It will not happen overnight. There are so many old habits that must be extinguished. Allow the Holy Spirit to renew in you a sense of organization. Allow Him to work in your heart, so that you can then work in your home and in the lives of your children.

As you progress toward a more organized lifestyle, you will be blessed. God will bless you with more time, more energy, and more peace. And with those three things you can finally do all that He has called you to do. Right now He's called you to teach your children. The time is now.

Additional Resources

GETTING ORGANIZED

Web Sites and Articles

The Big Picture of Other People. http://pages.prodigy.com/getolife/people.html

Identifying Stumbling Blocks on Your Road to Organization. http://pages.prodigy.com/getolife/mh3.html

Organize Your World. www.organizeyourworld.com

Habits of Being Clutter-Free. www.organized-living.com/articles

Organomics Tip of the Month. www.organomics.com

The Get Organized News. www.tgon.com

Books

Cheryl R. Carter. *Organize Your Life!* Uniondale, NY: Jehonadah Communications, 1999.

Ronnie Eisenberg and Kate Kelly. *Organize Yourself.* St. Paul: Hungry Minds, Inc., 1997.

Sandra Felton. *How Not to Be a Messie.* New York: Galahad Books, 1999.

Dorothy Lehmkuhland and Dolores Lamping. *Organizing for the Creative Person.* New York: Crown, 1994.

Bonnie McCullough. *Totally Organized.* New York: St. Martin's Press, 1986.

Julie Morgenstern. *Organizing from the Inside Out.* New York: Henry Holt & Co., Inc., 1998.

Robert Moskowitz. *How to Organize Your Work and Your Life.* New York: Main Street Books, 1981.

Pipi Campbell Peterson. *Ready, Set, Organize!* Indianapolis: JIST Works, 1995.

Valerie Titlow. *A Call to Organize.* Vista, CA: Organizers, 1992.

Dawn Walters and Helen Chislett. *Organized Living.* Wappingers Falls, NY: Antique Collectors Club, 1997.

Stephanie Winston. *Stephanie Winston's Best Organizing Tips.* New York: Simon & Schuster, 1995.

Pam Young and Peggy Jones. *Get Your Act Together.* New York: Harper Perennial, 1993.

ORGANIZING YOUR TIME

Web Sites and Articles

Time Management. www.organized-living.com/articles

Do's and Don'ts. www.clinique.com/archiveex/03.97/dos.html

Goal-setting. www.mindtools.com

Planning. www.mindtools.com

Time Management Skills. www.mindtools.com

Books

Stephanie Culp. *How to Get Organized When You Don't Have Time.* Cincinnati: Writers Digest Books, 1986.

Stephanie Culp. *Stephanie Culp's 12-Month Organizer and Project Planner.* Cincinnati: Betterway Books, 1995.

Ronnie Eisenberg and Kate Kelly. *The Overwhelmed Person's Guide to Time Management.* New York: Plume, 1997.

Roberta Roesch. *Time Management for Busy People.* New York: McGraw-Hill, 1998.

Dr. Jan Yager. *Creative Time Management.* Stamford Creek, CT: Hannacroix Creek Books, 1999.

ORGANIZING YOUR SPACE

Web Sites and Articles

Systems for Organized Lifestyles. www.organized-living.com/articles

Studio Apartment Solutions. www.stretcher.com

Pack Rat Space Planning. www.stretcher.com

Books

Anacaria Myrrha. *Systems by Design: The Practical Art of Personal Organization.* San Rafael, CA: Simple Systems, 1989.

Elizabeth Wilhide. *Creating Space.* San Francisco: Soma Books, 1998.

ORGANIZING YOUR SUPPLIES AND MATERIALS

Web Sites and Articles

To Save or Not to Save. www.organized-living.com/articles

1-2-3 Sort It: Residential Organizing. www.123Sortit.com

Creating More Storage Space. www.sirius.com/~lindah/frugal/storspce.html

Books

Don Aslett. *Clutter's Last Stand.* Cincinnati: Writers' Digest Books, 1984.

Emilie Barnes. *15 Minute Home and Family Organizer.* New York: Inspirational Press, 1998.

Sheree Bykofsky. *500 Terrific Ideas for Organizing Everything*. New York: Galahad Books, 1992.

Sally Clark. *House Beautiful Storage*. New York: Hearst Books, 1998.

Complete Home Storage, by Southern Living. Birmingham, AL: Oxmoor House, 1999.

Creating Storage. Menlo Park, CA: Sunset Books, 1995.

Stephanie Culp. *How to Conquer Clutter*. Cincinnati: Writers' Digest Books, 1989.

Stephanie Culp. *Organized Closets and Storage for Every Room in the House*. Cincinnati: Writers' Digest Books, 1990.

Ronnie Eisenberg and Kate Kelly. *Organize Your Home*. New York: Hyperion, 1999.

Richard Freudenberger. *Building Storage Stuff*. Asheville, NC: Lark Books, 1997.

Linda Hallam, ed. *301 Stylish Storage Ideas*. Des Moines, IA: Better Homes & Gardens Books, 1998.

Cynthia Inions. *The Storage Book*. New York: Abbeville Press, Inc., 1997.

Donna M. Murphy. *Organize Your Books in 6 Easy Steps*. Fort Collins, CO: IRIE Pub., 1998.

Maxine Ordesky. *The Complete Home Organizer*. New York: Grove Press, 1993.

Perfect Order. San Francisco: Soma Books, 1999.

ORGANIZING YOUR PAPERWORK

Web Sites and Articles

The Shoebox Method of Filing Papers. http://pages.prodigy.com/getolife/shoebox.html

Paper Training for Home Business. http://pages.prodigy.com/getolife/paper.html

Conquering Clutter. www.organized-living.com/articles

Paper Management. www.organized-living.com/articles

Paper Clutter. www.web-oats.com/clutterbug

Books

Stephanie Culp. *Conquering the Paper Pile Up*. Cincinnati: Writers' Digest Books, 1990.

Barbara Hemphill. *Taming the Paper Tiger at Home*. Washington, D.C.: Kiplinger Times Bus., 1997.

Index

158 THE ORGANIZED HOMESCHOOLER